B- Bell, Alexander Graham
Eber, Dorothy Harley
    Genius at work

K

DATE DUE

MAY 22 2008

GAYLORD   PRINTED IN U.S.A.

GENIUS AT WORK

GENIUS AT WORK

Images of Alexander Graham Bell

Dorothy Harley Eber

A STUDIO BOOK

The Viking Press   New York

For Vera Williams Harley, and in loving memory of
George Ernest Esmond Harley, who first told me stories of Nova Scotia

Copyright © 1982 by Dorothy Harley Eber

First published in 1982 by The Viking Press
625 Madison Avenue, New York, N.Y. 10022

Library of Congress Cataloging in Publication Data
Eber, Dorothy.
  Genius at work.
  (A Studio book)
  Bibliography: p.
  1. Bell, Alexander Graham, 1847–1922.   2. Inventors—
United States—Biography.   I. Title.
TK6143.B4E23   621.385′092′4 [B]   81–11670
ISBN 0–670–27389–9   AACR2

Printed in the United States of America
Set in Baskerville
Designed by Michael Shroyer

Contents

Acknowledgments

My first thanks must go to those persons who knew Alexander Graham Bell and his family and generously shared their memories with me. This book began as a result of conversations I had with Mayme Morrison Brown and grew as I met others who had first-hand memories of the great inventor. I am indebted to them for many happy hours and for the glimpses they afforded me of a mind that helped shape our century. All of their names appear in this book.

Much assistance was provided during the writing of this book by personnel of various Canadian and U.S. institutions and government departments. I would like to offer a special thank-you to Beverly Brannan, curator of the photographic collections in the Prints and Photographs Division of the Library of Congress, Washington, D.C., whose knowledge of the range of the Gilbert H. Grosvenor Collection of Alexander Graham Bell Photographs was of the greatest help, and to Richard Lindo, historian with the National Historic Parks and Sites Branch, Parks Canada, Ottawa, who kindly gave the manuscript a scholarly reading, advised on the interpretation of material in the Alexander Graham Bell papers, and helped with the verification of many facts. Any errors, of course, are my own. I would also like to thank Elizabeth Quance for assistance in locating information both in the library of the Alexander Graham Bell National Historic Park, Baddeck, and at Parks Canada, Ottawa, and for generously giving me access to her paper, prepared for Parks Canada, on "Alexander Graham Bell and the Tetrahedral Space Frame." This excellent study made clear for me many points in Bell's development of his revolutionary concept.

In Cape Breton, for generous assistance, I must thank John W. Stephens and the staff of the Alexander Graham Bell National Historic Park, and personnel of the Beaton Institute of Cape Breton Studies, a splendid source of information on the history and lore of Cape Breton. The book has benefited also from the discovery of a collection of papers of the late C. W. K. McCurdy, brought to my attention by Estelle MacRae, owner of the Red-

Frontispiece:
Alexander Graham Bell, his eldest grandson, Melville Grosvenor, and Cape Breton assistants haul on the rope of one of his experimental tetrahedral kites.
Opposite page:
Still hauling. (Both, Gilbert Grosvenor, 1908)

7

wood Antiques, at Nyanza, a few miles outside Baddeck. For assistance in collecting oral history relating to the flight of the *Silver Dart* I am indebted to Air Canada.

During preparation of the text and photographs for publication, perceptive and wise counseling and also encouragement came from my editors at Viking, Mary Velthoven and Amy Pershing. In addition, a number of persons advised on technical points and made helpful suggestions. I would like to thank Merloyd Lawrence, another summer resident of Nova Scotia, whose interest furthered work on this book from the beginning; Dr. Walter Hitschfeld, vice principal and dean of graduate studies; McGill University; Stanley Triggs, curator of the Notman Photographic Archives, McCord Museum; Tom Humphrey, archives technician; and Alan and Jane Fagan, Henry Strub, Gloria Pierre, and Lesley Andrassy. My thanks also to Ann Gill and Robin Fitzgerald, who typed the manuscript.

Since I first undertook this project, some four years ago, my husband, George F. Eber, has participated in countless conversations on matters relating to this book and has made literally hundreds of helpful comments. I thank him for his important contribution. Finally, it seems more than appropriate to express thanks to the Bell descendants who have generously placed the rich collection of Alexander Graham Bell papers with its great human interest in the public domain.

Dorothy Harley Eber
Montreal, 1981

Prologue: An Interview with R. Buckminster Fuller

Q. It seems to me that Bell's tetrahedron, which he developed while working on kites, is very like your geodesic structure?

A. Exactly the same.

Q. When you developed your structures, did you know about the work of Alexander Graham Bell?

A. I did not. I was astonished to learn about it later. It is the way nature behaves, so we both discovered nature. It isn't something you invent. You discover. I had the great advantage of being allowed to look through all of his notes in Washington at the National Geographic [Society]. His grandson had me admitted to his beautiful notebooks and I found where he comes to the actual discovering of it. The thing he was interested in was how to make a stronger aeroplane wing. He was probably taken with Langley [aviation pioneer Samuel Pierpont Langley] and all the others and he was trying to understand how he might do something better. And he comes to discovering omni-triangulation. I call it the octahedron-tetrahedron truss. Then of course he went right on with his kites but I knew absolutely nothing about it until I had discovered the same thing myself.

Of course I knew about Alexander Graham Bell discovering the telephone from my childhood. That was a great childhood event. I was born in 1895 and I remember the great excitement over the telephone. My Boston suburb home telephone number was "Milton Ten." So Alexander Graham Bell's name was very prominent in my life, but it occurred only in relation to the telephone. I'd been at what I discovered possibly fifteen years before somebody said, "Didn't you know Alexander Graham Bell did it?"

I didn't learn about Bell until after the geodesic dome, and the geodesic dome comes quite a long time after what I call the synergetic mathematics—the way the spheres of the unit radius close-pack. You just take two spheres and they just touch one another—that's all. You nest a third one down between the two and you get a triangle. Then you nest another on top and you get a tetrahedron. If now you take two triangular sets of three unit-radius spheres and nest one on top of the other, you will make an

Melville Grosvenor takes a ride on a kite rope. (Gilbert Grosvenor, 1908)

octahedron unit. If you finally make two layers of spheres in closest packing, the spheres are the vertexes of the octahedron-tetrahedral truss. Many such closest-packed, unit-radius sphere layers, nested upon one another, produce the vertexes of what is known in physics as the "isotropic vector matrix." I've discovered it is the way atoms are packing. So it seems to be fundamental to nature. Absolutely fundamental to nature.

My first objective structural experimenting occurred in my pre-eyeglass, blurred-vision, 1899 kindergarten. The teacher gave us equilength toothpicks and semidried peas. She told us to make structures—houses. All the other children, none of whom had eye trouble, put together rectilinear box houses. The peas were strong enough to act as angle-holding gussets. Not having visualized the rectilinearity about me, I used only my tactile sense. My finger muscles found that only the triangle had a natural shape-holding capability. I therefore felt my way into producing an octahedron-tetrahedron truss assembly. I, of course, knew naught of such names.

I can remember the teacher, Miss Williams, asking other teachers to come and look at the strange structure I had produced. Fifty years later I heard from that teacher, who clearly remembered that strange event. Just two years ago her grandniece spoke to me, telling me of her great-aunt's death and of her great-aunt's remembering that 1899 event to the end. It was this experience which undoubtedly started me off at fifteen to look for nature's own structural coordinate system.

Q. When you were a boy, did you think of Bell as a sort of universal genius?

A. I only knew about the telephone. The way I was being educated and the amount of news that really got around in those days was pretty loose, and I didn't have any idea about his being the kind of really great scientist he is. When I had the privilege once of his notebooks, I just marveled. . . . His notebooks are almost like the Leonardo books.

From an interview with Dorothy Harley Eber, on the telephone, June 29, 1978

The winged boat, one of Bell's early tetrahedral kites, was "raised in the air by attaching it to a galloping horse," as Bell wrote beside this picture in his album. (George McCurdy, November 19, 1902)

Arrivals

"Anytime you went down Beinn Bhreagh road at Red Head, Dr. Bell had kites flying. It was beautiful in the air. Sometimes, depending on the wind, they would move back and forth and up and down like any ordinary little kites. But he was testing all the time, trying to get something lighter than air, experimenting with the tetrahedron. That's why he flew those kites. He was really trying to get a machine that would fly."

That's Mayme Morrison Brown talking the day this book began.

The picture changes when you cross the causeway; here on Nova Scotia's Cape Breton Island the image you've brought from the mainland of Alexander Graham Bell—elderly, genial, constantly talking into the telephone—begins to disappear. Here in the town of Baddeck, where the great inventor sometimes spent half of each year, people rarely mention the telephone. They may report that he answered the phone with "Hoy, hoy"—never hello; that he told his grandchildren, "It's for calling out, not for calling in." But that's all. Instead, they tell you about his "cigar boat," the fastest ship in the world, or how he scoured the island for six-nippled sheep, or built the world's first space frame and pioneered flight with red silk kites.

It's an appealing portrait. In no time I found that I liked Baddeck's Alexander Graham Bell better than the one on the mainland. "He makes you feel," said his houseguest Helen Keller in 1901, "if you only had a little more time, you too might be an inventor." It raised the spirits to think of Bell, the great generalist, now that everyone's a specialist. Even I, a journalist, write more and more about a single subject.

Of course, I did not originally come to Cape Breton to discover Alexander Graham Bell. I came to buy a house by the sea, on the shores that encircle the wonderful saltwater Bras d'Or lakes. Cape Breton has a lovely, rugged, and wild countryside that often makes people think of Scotland and for about one hundred years Baddeck has been a summer place for Americans who don't mind the longish journey. But I was in Baddeck only two minutes before I knew whose country this was.

Opposite page:
Detail of a photograph of Alexander Graham Bell taken about 1907 by Mayme Morrison Brown.

I checked into the Telegraph House Motel, where Gussie McInnes at the desk said, "We'll put you in Dr. Bell's room." She showed me up the stairs of the old inn (the motel is a recent addition) to the blue-and-white room—complete with spool beds and old-fashioned crockery—where Alexander Graham Bell did indeed stay with his wife on his first fateful visit in 1885. When I complained that Dr. Bell's room was drafty, Gussie said, "We'll move you out of Number One into Number Two; he won't mind."

The telephone was nine years old when the Bells, on a visit from Washington, D.C., came to Baddeck. They were young and rich and looking for a summer place. Bell himself was thirty-eight; Mabel, his highly intelligent, independently wealthy, and deaf wife, was ten years younger. Already they were immortal. She was the girl, it says on a family picture, for whom the telephone had been invented; he was the great inventor. Not long before, the London *Times* had called him a "black whiskered young crank" and the phone itself "American hum-bug," but already the "wire toy" had linked the world. Individuals, business, government had rushed to test his patent, but his claim to the most valuable single patent ever issued remained secure. For thirty-seven years, a fraction short of half of his life, dug in among the Scots settlers, Bell worked in the summer laboratory he set up here—and never stopped experimenting, inventing, and discovering. As he put it, "There seems to be always something going where I am. Nothing, perhaps, that would interest other people, but it keeps me busy and interested all the time."

Between trips around the Cape Breton countryside looking for my perfect house, I sat downstairs in the Telegraph House parlor amid the warm wood and comfortable Victoriana. One day Geraldine Dunlop Jackson, a granddaughter of the original owner and a sister of Buddy Dunlop, who with his wife, Mary, runs the inn today, told me the story as it has been passed down in her family of the Bells' first visit to Baddeck. They were on their way to Newfoundland and had stopped in Cape Breton to look at coal mines in which Mabel's father, Gardiner Greene Hubbard, had an interest. They made a side trip to Baddeck.

"In those days the only way of coming into Baddeck was by boat," Geraldine Jackson explained. "To come to Baddeck you always had to go to Iona and then come across by ferry. In my time the hotel always sent a car to pick up the passengers at the wharf, but in my grandfather's day I guess they sent the horse and buggy. Dr. Bell had read that book by Dudley Warner, *Baddeck and That Sort of Thing,* which mentioned our place. So he asked for our place and came up and stayed in Number One."

Baddeck lighthouse and schooners,
about 1915. (Notman Studios)

15

Baddeck and That Sort of Thing, by Charles Dudley Warner, was published in 1874. Warner, a friend of Bell's, had written: "Let the reader not understand that we are recommending him to go to Baddeck. . . . There are few whom it would pay to go a thousand miles for the sake of sitting on the dock at Baddeck when the sun goes down. . . . You can see all that as well elsewhere? I am not so sure. There is a harmony about the Bras d'Or at Baddeck which is lacking in many scenes of more pretension."

"The room was exactly the same—those were the beds," explained Geraldine, "and the hotel is just the same, except in those days they didn't have running water. The hotel had its own reservoir out in the back field and when Dr. Bell stayed here there were outhouses. I've seen pictures . . . five in a row for ladies and five for men.

"They were here on a weekend, and my grandfather David and my grandmother Isobel took them for a Sunday afternoon drive in the buggy, the double-seater, from the inn over to the Point, and Dr. Bell fell in love with Beinn Bhreagh. They came back in the summer and Dr. Bell bought the first part, I think, where he built the big house and then just kept adding to it by buying farms."

In time, much of the population of Victoria County became involved in the experiments Bell conducted there on the Point. The record of this mutual effort is now quite grandly housed in the museum of the Alexander Graham Bell National Historic Park, just past the center of town.

One morning early in my visit I wandered over there. I found myself drawn back again and again by the extraordinary photographs, some taken by family members and friends, many by Bell's son-in-law Dr. Gilbert H. Grosvenor, first editor of the *National Geographic* (which Bell helped found and was largely responsible for casting in its present form), others the work of little-known Cape Bretoners who photographed, developed, and printed at Bell's behest.

The pictures show Bell using his whole headland and Baddeck Bay as a launching ground for giant kites. He is helped by Mabel, various grandchildren, Cape Breton workmen, and, in some, by a quartet of eager young men drawn to the experiments by the magnetism of the man who invented the telephone and by the chance to "get into the air," to be in on the breakthrough in "flying machines." In these big blowups Bell appears as a huge, larger-than-life figure, dressed in tweeds. ("He always wore those knickerbockers and he looked so stately," remembers Freddie Pinaud, whose father ran Bell's boatyard.) The pictures take you on a

Opposite page:
Mabel and Alexander Graham Bell with their daughters, Elsie May and Marian (Daisy), in 1885, the year of their first visit to Baddeck.

17

Left:
Approaching Baddeck.
Below:
Chebucto Street, Baddeck, with
the promontory of Red Head in
the background. (Both from Mabel
Bell's album. About 1890)

nostalgic trip back to the days when "snapshotting" and telephoning were spreading like wildfire, as well as into the home laboratories where modern technology was born.

There are rare early pictures that show Bell as a tall, thin young man with a very black beard. In 1870, fifteen years before he arrived in Baddeck, Bell and his father and mother left Scotland for Canada after two brothers had died of TB. Like his father he worked as a speech therapist and specialized in teaching the deaf. He began teaching in Boston, and six years later patented the telephone. But the telephone had its earliest beginning in his efforts to develop a device to help deaf people. In his experiments—he used human ears taken from cadavers—Bell glimpsed the essence of the telephone. He was then twenty-seven years old.

One day in the museum library I dipped into photocopies of the Bell papers. There were family letters. All the Bells and everyone connected with them wrote furiously—even the butler. "I wooed you with my pen," Bell once reminded Mabel. Despite the telephone, as Mabel Bell's last secretary, Polly MacMechan Dobson, points out, it was the age of letter writing. There are also shelves of Bell's own in-house newsletter, the *Beinn Bhreagh Recorder,* which he circulated among friends and associates. And shelves of astonishing notebooks. Bell's faithfulness of notation was remarkable, Buckminster Fuller told me later. Each day's train of thought and activity was noted down. These notebooks record that after the telephone and his communication achievements, Bell also made contributions in medicine, genetics, eugenics, aviation, and marine navigation. Much that characterizes our age is here in embryo—along with such asides as how to rig up a good ghost and how to build a composting toilet.

But off Cape Breton Island, how widely known were these achievements? Was I the only one out there who had never heard of Bell the aviation pioneer?

The Bell archives are overflowing. There's plenty there to change the old image.

In one letter written by Bell during the early years of his marriage while he was away testifying at one of the great telephone patent suits that troubled him for years, there seems a suggestion that he feared the type of fame that was to engulf him.

"Oh! Mabel dear—please please PLEASE (that's copied from you) make me write. Make me describe and publish my ideas that I may at least obtain credit for them and that people may know that I am still alive and working and thinking. I can't bear to hear that even my friends should think that I stumbled upon an invention and that there is no more good in me."

At that time Bell was absorbed in work on the photophone, a

device that made use of a focused beam of sunlight to transmit the spoken word. Bell always contended that this was his great discovery, outranking in potential importance even the telephone. No one believed him; the sun does not always shine and so the photophone was not practical. Bell and his associates turned in a new direction, pioneering in the development of the wax phonograph record and securing valuable patents in connection with it. But the photophone's day did arrive: in 1957 Charles Townes and Arthur Schawlow developed the laser for Bell Laboratories and in 1977 the Bell System, using the amplified light of the laser and the technology of fiber optics, installed under the streets of Chicago the first communications system to carry phone calls, computer data, and video signals on pulses of light.

The real-estate agent who drove me around the countryside while I searched for a house was Kenny MacDermid. It turned out that Kenny had grown up at Beinn Bhreagh; his father, John, had been the Bell coachman. Kenny was also manager of the Bell properties, and one day after we'd been out looking, he drove me through the estate grounds. As we passed the big house, he pointed out the kitchen window against which Bell threw stones the time he went swimming and lost his clothes, and the outdoor sleeping porch that was the Bell bedroom. A great-grandson sometimes sleeps there now, and I noticed a Vasarely poster on the wall. I learned that at one time the family had opened the house to visitors, and according to Norman Bethune, who owned the local hire car, Bell himself welcomed all comers, even reporters. But although today up to three thousand visitors tour the Alexander Graham Bell National Historic Park daily, the Beinn Bhreagh grounds are off limits. I knew I'd had a rare treat.

Finally, after inspecting waterside properties (too expensive) and abandoned one-room schools (too remote), I found a small, shingled farmhouse with a mansard roof at the top of Crescent Grove, a country road that ends in a plateau with a broad blue view of the Bras d'Or. When they searched the title it turned out that the land on which my house stands had once belonged to Alexander Graham Bell. With his eye on the headland across the bay, he had lived here in another farmhouse, now gone. While his agent and secretary Arthur McCurdy bought for him, parcel by parcel, the land on the opposite point that then belonged to the McAulay family, Bell renovated and enlarged the old farmhouse to meet the needs of his family.

"It's too bad you missed Charlie," people said when I expressed interest in the history of my property. "He kept such beautiful records." The late C. W. K. McCurdy—kin to Arthur—had been, I discovered, for many years Baddeck's town clerk; he was

Staff and students of the Boston
School for the Deaf, June 21, 1871.
Alexander Graham Bell, one year
out from Edinburgh, is at top
right.

Bell's photophone and the transmission of articulate speech over a beam of light are shown in two 1880 illustrations. Application of the principle of the photophone became possible with the development of modern laser and fiber optics technology.

also a member of the numerous and prominent McCurdy family that had been closely involved with the Bells. And he did keep beautiful records. In 1947 Charlie published his memories of Alexander Graham Bell in installments of *The Monthly Bulletin,* the employees' magazine of the Maritime Telegram & Telephone Association & Associate Companies, Halifax. In these memoirs Charlie McCurdy wrote:

"One summer about the middle of the 1880s a very delightful family came to live in a house next door, on the western side, to my father's house at Crescent Grove, Baddeck, Nova Scotia. This was the family of Alexander Graham Bell—Mr. and Mrs. Bell and their two very nice little girls.

"Their house was a one and one-half story building, which the following year they had lifted up into the air and another full story built underneath, thus making the house a full two and one-half stories high. I remember the whole proceeding, as it appeared a wonderful thing that anyone could lift a whole house so high and put another set of four or five large rooms underneath it . . .

"About this time the Bells built a large barn just behind the house, a very fine barn indeed . . . In this barn was a very nice living apartment for the Negro coachman whose name was Parent. There was also in the barn a section where Mr. Bell conducted certain experiments, such perhaps as his earliest thoughts of air travel. I remember seeing in this section a circular platform of light wood, sitting on small supports, through the centre of which passed a long straight pole or stick from floor to ceiling. Around the edge of this circular platform were a number of small propellers connected each to an electric wire which in turn was connected to a battery which I think Parent kept manipulating or pumping. The propellers would then spin around creating a vacuum over the small platform which would then be pushed up the pole by the air pressure beneath, or drawn into the vacuum thus created above the platform.

"Douglas McCurdy, who worked and lived with Mr. Bell for many years in later days, tells me that this could not have happened previous to the building of Mr. Bell's laboratory on the other side of the Bay, a few years later. However, I saw the experiment as just described, in the barn . . .

"When the Bells first came to live in the Crescent Grove house next to my home, my mother, taking with her my brother Bertie and myself, drove over to the Bells' front gate in our phaeton and took the two little girls for a drive. They were very small and pretty. Upon my mother's asking them their names, one said, 'My name is Elsie May Bell and my birthday is in May.' The

Above:
Neighbors called the Bells' first Baddeck house, on Crescent Grove, the "house on stilts" after it was jacked up to add a new first story. (From Mabel Bell's album, about 1890)

Left:
"Fascinate your artist as much as you can," Bell wrote to Mabel on April 5, 1879, "lay regular siege to his heart—in order that those beautiful eyes and sweet face that I value so much may grow out of the canvas . . . I wish I were an artist. My goodness! Wouldn't I paint a picture that would astonish you!"

other said, 'My name is Marian Hubbard Bell but they call me Daisy.' . . .

"We children all played together every day. One day I said I would take one of them on horseback to water the horses at the brook about a quarter mile north of our house, but as the horses were watered very early in the morning whoever came would have to come early. Sure enough, early next morning the younger of the two girls got up very quietly and crawled through a broken window. . . . However, the man in charge of the horses wouldn't let either of us go with him that morning, fearing that something might happen, so we missed that looked-forward-to adventure . . .

"I remember that during Mr. Bell's study of the air currents in those early days he would sometimes send up into the air over Baddeck Bay at night dozens of large coloured paper balloons, fashioned in many shapes such as giant men, horses, cows, elephants, etc., and lighted and glowing. What a delight it was to us young people, or for that matter to everyone else in the place, old and young, to see those lighted men and animals floating in the sky on a calm night, high and low in all directions, sometimes passing each other, perhaps dipping in a bow as they passed, according to as the varying air currents took them. Never had such a sight been seen in Cape Breton, until Mr. Bell carried on his air current investigations in the calm darkness of a warm summer night."

Despite this splendid memoir, I found I still missed Charlie. There are excellent books on Bell's scientific achievements, but Charlie's account was firsthand—and tantalizing. I wanted more. What was the great inventor really like? People like Charlie *knew*. Charlie was dead, but there were people still living who had memories of Bell and the way he worked. As I settled in as a summer resident I began to hope I might meet some of them.

Often in the summer evenings I'd walk down Crescent Grove toward the bay over which Bell had sent up the glowing lights. I'd call on my neighbors J. D. and Anna Smith in their old farmhouse near the shore. J.D.'s father had worked for the Bells, and as a child J.D. had lived for a time at the farm on the Bell estate. A plumbing contractor, J.D. now works regularly on the *Elsie,* the yacht with the red sails that has sometimes appeared in the *National Geographic.* J.D. watched it being launched from Bell's boatyard in 1919. As I drank coffee and ate oatmeal cookies, J.D. and Anna would show me pictures of old Baddeck. Then, as now, religion and politics were passionate concerns. The community when the Bells arrived was larger than it is today and apparently colorful; the sleighs in winter would line up outside Mother Gaelic's and the other bootleggers on Water Street. We talked of the way

25

Bell's presence had touched people's lives, of the jobs he had brought to this country of chronic unemployment, but even more of the excitement his adventures had engendered and how for a period of years the people here had gone adventuring with him.

One day J.D. said, "You ought to talk to Mayme."

During our first phone conversation Mary Morrison Brown did not take too kindly to the suggestion that her experiences were part of history and ought to be in books. "History! I want to tell you I keep as far away from history as I can," said Mayme, who was born in 1892. But eventually, armed with my tape recorder, I walked the few blocks from the center of town to where Mayme's well-appointed trailer was parked and she met me at the door— tall, vital, quick of mind, and warm in welcome. Inside, seated on Mayme's sofa, I threw her a curveball. Would Dr. Bell have envisaged the tape recorder?* "Probably," said Mayme. "He thought of most things."

On a plaque on the museum wall I found Bell's credo: "The inventor is a man who looks around upon the world, and is not contented with things as they are. He wants to improve whatever he sees, he wants to benefit the world; he is haunted by an idea, the spirit of invention possesses him, seeking materialisation."

Sometimes, when I glance at the plaque on visits to the museum, I wonder if the generalist "who looks around" could still make meaningful discoveries today. Aren't inventions in the age of High Tech made in the research departments of great corporations, in the minds of highly qualified specialists? Isn't it scientific know-how alone that leads to great discoveries? It's satisfying to reflect that Albert Einstein did not think so. "When I examine myself and my methods of thought," he told a friend, "I come to the conclusion that the gift of fantasy has meant more to me than my talent for absorbing positive knowledge." Buckminster Fuller rails against the specialist. Speaking chiefly to specialists—planners, architects, and engineers—in *Operating Manual for Spaceship Earth* Fuller says that mankind's survival depends on *comprehensive* thinking. Computers can supply the specialized thinking.

Will the generalist gain a new lease on life in the age of High Tech?

Will he keep us human in the computer age?

---

* Robert V. Bruce in *Bell: Alexander Graham Bell and the Conquest of Solitude* notes that while developing the phonograph record, Bell and his associates in 1881 conceived the idea "of impressing on the record a permanent magnetic field, varying from point to point, which would produce sound as a pickup of some kind traversed it—the embryo, in short, of modern tape recording."

In the same year, family members enjoy a pleasant summer's day with Bell.

Bell poses alone. (Photographs from Mabel Bell's album)

27

Above:
The *Blue Hill* at Baddeck wharf, with passengers embarking for Sydney, Nova Scotia.
Right, above:
Baddeck from the wharf. (Both, Notman Studios, 1912–1916)
Right:
"Grace and her children, Crescent Grove wharf," Mabel wrote beside this picture, taken about 1890. Across the water are Red Head and the Bell property.

A meeting outside the Baddeck
courthouse. Political and religious
sentiment ran high among Cape
Breton's strong-minded Scots settlers. (Notman Studios, 1912–1916)

The Inventor at Home

Except for the "terrible distance from Washington," Alexander
Graham Bell and Mabel decided on first sight that Cape Breton
offered all they had sought during ten years' travels up and down
the Atlantic seaboard. They climbed to the top of the high penin-
sula that juts into the salt Bras d'Or water across from Baddeck
and at the summit decided to buy the point if possible. Perhaps as
they came down again they had a sense that the mountain was
fated, preordained to be theirs. Years later Mabel Bell recalled
that there had been a dramatic encounter: as they, the "incoming
new masters," walked down the hill, "the past old master Donald
McAulay was being borne forth from his house for the last time
. . . to rest in the little graveyard on the hillside."

Donald McAulay was Mayme Morrison Brown's great-uncle.
After the Bells secured their point, buying property from the
McAulay heirs as well as from others, an extraneous farm, a mem-
orandum by Mabel Bell records, "was sold under mortgage to
Mrs. Morrison" (Mayme's mother). By an odd quirk of fate, Mrs.
Mary Morrison's uncle was Alexander Graham of Edinburgh, in
all probability the same man whom Bell, christened simply
Alexander, admired so much in boyhood that he chose to add the
older man's surname to his own. "He told me he knew Alexander
well—and liked him so much," Mayme remembered. "Alexander
was something to do with the army, and he had been to the
Caribbean. All the old Scottish people knew each other."

Mayme grew up as a next-door neighbor, working for Bell in
his laboratory during some of its most exciting days and later, in
order to "travel a bit," working in the Bell household. "In Washington Mrs. Bell and I discussed whether I should become a nurse,
but I didn't want to be a nurse; I'd rather have been a doctor." In
fact Mayme had other plans. In 1914, just before World War I
broke out, she married Jack MacKenzie and bore four children.
Baddeck people who were children when Mayme was a young
married woman told me she had been beautiful, wore nice clothes,
and was quite well off. "She had those big hats and was the first
woman in Cape Breton to own her own roadster," one remem-

31

bered. Widowed in 1928, Mayme was married again in 1935 this time to Daniel Brown, who was later killed in the "Princess Trip," an infamous Cape Breton mine disaster.

You'll never catch Mayme in a rocking chair. ("Sitting in one is like worrying—you rock and rock and don't get anywhere.") But slowed down now by arthritis, through many a summer afternoon she rested in a roomy chair while I sat opposite and listened as she told me about "Dr. Bell and the crazy things he used to do."

There's probably no one alive today who remembers the great inventor further back—or has better qualifications for reminiscing. Mayme last saw and talked to Bell just weeks before he died,

Bell in a photograph taken by Mayme Morrison Brown about 1907.

when she and her mother went down to the Point House and sat with him on the veranda.

"Some of the old people thought the man was foolish to spend so much time flying kites. 'It seems like a damn fool thing to do,' they'd say. And I can hear Dr. Bell laugh yet when he heard that. He'd throw back his head and his whiskers would bounce. 'They think I'm some kind of nut,' he'd say. 'You're a *useful* nut,' I'd tell him. They'd classified him as one.

"Opinionated? The old people? I'll say! In those days you were either a Grit or a Tory. They'd get together in the evenings and they'd get so cross! When he advanced some, they realized he was doing something but, then, they thought an airplane was an awful thing. A man taking a chance in the air! He'd be killed for sure. There are not too many of the old people left. I doubt if there are any. Those families in Red Head and Baddeck and Big Harbour are all gone. I'm the only one left who worked in the laboratory.

"I'm not going to tell you how old I am. Women don't like to tell. I worked in the laboratory in 1905. I just went down for a lark. I was thirteen—I'd got to grade ten. Just went down and started doing a little bit of everything. I started doing the little cells—the tetrahedral cells. We used to pile up hundreds for the big kites . . . the *Frost King* and the *Cygnet* and all those. . . . They're probably somewhere cluttered in the museum down there. They were there a few years ago.

"The first time I went through the Alexander Graham Bell Museum here in Baddeck after it was built, the director, Kielor Bentley, was there. He wondered who the old lady was who just glanced at things, she didn't bother looking at them. He said, 'I'm trying to find out who the people are in those pictures.'

"So I told him all about the pictures, not knowing he was wishing he had caught me with a recorder. 'Come over and have coffee,' he said. And I said, 'If you put a spike in it I will some day.' He did ask me but there were so many, each giving a different version, that I didn't want to get mixed up in it. Most people would tell you something they thought or had heard about him. I grew up with them and I used to get right mad.

"My sister and I were born and raised in Beinn Bhreagh— that's Gaelic for 'Beautiful Mountain.' Dr. Bell named it Beinn Bhreagh, but the whole section over there is Red Head. It was always Red Head because when the first settlers—my people—came sailing through the lakes here the first thing they saw was the big red rock. They called it Red Head and they settled there. That was a long, long time ago.

"My mother's people, my great-grandparents, sold their prop-

Mayme Morrison Brown at about sixteen. (Detail from a 1907 photograph)

erty to Dr. Bell. At first Mother told me they didn't want to sell, but the young people had all gone away. They sold to McCurdy and McCurdy did the business for Dr. Bell. Dr. Bell's granddaughter says she still has the lilacs my great-great-grandfather planted. Then before I was born my family bought a property and built there. But my father didn't go fishing or farming here; he was a prospector and miner. He went out to California and was killed. So I grew up with the family. I saw them every day.

"Dr. Bell loved down there. Sometimes he'd stay until March. Then he'd go back to Washington for a month or two for business reasons and to entertain some, and come right back. He would have lived here all the time if he could. He loved Beinn Bhreagh. Didn't he hate to put on a dress suit! 'Don't I hate Washington,' he'd say, 'where I have to have this cardboard on.' You know they had those starched shirt fronts . . . he didn't like a tie. He always wore those knickerbockers. He thought he was dressed up in those.

"He was down in the lab, he was in his study, and weekends he spent in the houseboat [*Mabel of Beinn Bhreagh*]. Nice little place . . . kitchen, sleeping quarters and everything. We called it Dr. Bell's floating palace. When the Bells first came down here, they used to be towed all over the lakes in it . . . Washabuck, Marble Mountain. . . . When they quit gallivanting they got the men to haul it above the beach into the pond. Dr. Bell would go down on Friday and he wouldn't come home until Monday.

"Dr. Bell always came to Mother's and Mrs. Bell did, too. My first memory of Dr. Bell is of walking down from our house at Red Head with him to the road where his carriage was waiting. He was going to make me walk, but I couldn't make it. He had to pick me up and carry me. I remember him often taking me in his arms when I was little.

"He was a great big man, Dr. Bell. Black eyes . . . like an actor's. They'd go right through you and a lot of people were scared of him. I don't know why . . . they were cheerful eyes . . . they'd sparkle. Unless he was serious. If anything worried him, his eyes changed. His eyes weren't alive. If you saw a frown on his forehead and his eyes right black, there was something bothering him. But most of the time he'd be laughing.

"He told me one time he could mesmerize me. He probably could . . . to a certain extent. If you kept looking, his eyes were very penetrating. But he'd do a lot of things just from badness. One day he said, 'Mary dear, come right here. Watch me mesmerize the hen.' I couldn't have been more than ten or eleven. He went out on the front porch and he drew a big circle with a piece of chalk, put the hen in there and swung it around and said, 'See her! She won't go by that line. I've got her mesmerized!' He was teasing. He didn't know I knew anything about poultry! He'd turned the hen around so often she was dizzy. He was full of those things. He liked to have a joke on anyone. He was always tormenting someone. His sister-in-law Cassie used to say, 'Do you ever mind Alexander?' I'd say, 'No, I never pay any attention to him. I'm not sensible enough to pick up on him.' Oh, he was a grand person."

The stereotyped image I had carried from "the mainland" began to fade when I first came to Baddeck and it disappeared quickly after I began to talk to Mayme. Bell's younger daughter, Marian—known to all as Daisy—continued my education.

Left, below:
Marian Bell, usually called Daisy, was born in 1880.
Below:
Her older sister, Elsie May, was born in 1878.

Daisy was born at the time her father invented the photo-phone through which he heard a "ray of sun laugh and cough and sing!" When she was twenty-one, he wrote to congratulate her, calling her "our photophone in the truest and highest sense."

In 1905 Daisy married David Fairchild, who worked for the U.S. Department of Agriculture as an agricultural explorer. Along with others Fairchild helped develop the Florida citrus industry by introducing new varieties of citrus fruits.

All the Bells took up the pen with the greatest alacrity—but none with greater verve than Daisy Bell Fairchild. After the Bells' deaths, she, like other family members and friends, put down her memories of her parents in notes, apparently to smooth the way for an eventual biographer.

"As a child I can remember how he would speculate on just what a scientific man, cast ashore on an uninhabited island with only a penknife and his watch, would do to keep alive. With the *Mabel of Beinn Bhreagh* on its lonely bit of beach, he felt at least that he could find out.

"So one day, armed with his penknife, he started off in search of food. The most promising things he found were the heads of ripe seeds of one of the big weeds growing in his freshwater pond.

Bell driving along the shore on Sable Island, looking for the wreckage of a ship in which friends had lost their lives. (Arthur McCurdy, 1898)

These he collected and ate, along with some partridge berries, but didn't find them very sustaining. His search for clothing wasn't much more successful. Realistically he started off stark naked, again with his penknife. He cut the long flexible roots of some young spruce trees and with these bound sphagnum moss to his body—but the moss was damp and he decided the scientific man would get on better in some other climate than Canada!"

Bell's love of nature is a theme repeated in many of Daisy's reminiscences: "Father was a most elemental person, a creature of water and the woods and the night. He would float about in the water by the hour, particularly at night, smoking a cigar and looking up at the stars. . . . I don't know just when his love of the night originated and I think it had many causes. He learned to work at night because he needed absolute quiet and the knowledge that he would not be interrupted in order to think and probably the same reason led him to walk alone so much at night. I think also the fact of his eyes being very sensitive to light made him crave the darkness. . . .

"Almost any night Father might start off, for a midnight walk, clad in bathing suit and shoes, but if there were a storm on, nothing could hold him in the house—and the harder the rain, the more he loved it. Snow he loved too. I shall never forget the boyish glee with which he told me one morning of the fun he had had fighting his way through a snowdrift with only his bathing suit and arctics on.

"One of the funniest things that ever happened to Father came about through this—I don't know what to call it—this urge to mingle with the universe . . .

"On the day of which I speak Mother had gone to Baddeck early in the evening to the Club, and Father started off to walk down to the houseboat. When he was about halfway down there, the lure of the starlit water was too much for him, so he left the road and walked down a little path to the water's edge where he undressed, left his clothes and started off along the shore, sometimes wading, sometimes swimming when the rocks jutted out too far.

"But it was longer to go than he thought and he was tired and chilled when he arrived and glad to roll up in a blanket and go to sleep. How long he slept of course he didn't know, but when he did wake up he didn't feel at all like going back through the cold water, so he walked along the road instead—but for the life of him he couldn't find the path down which he had gone and at the end of which he had left his clothes!

"He walked back almost to the house, then turned around, hoping to recognize the place when he approached it from the same direction, but no, he just couldn't find that path. And meantime there he was, getting colder every minute.

"At last he decided that he couldn't stay in the road all night and he'd have to try for the house; the house is set on a hill with two grass terraces in front, then a sloping lawn ending in a fringe of trees. Along the fringe of trees slunk poor Father, watching the moving figures in the brightly lighted house and darting across the shafts of light that came out from the windows.

"Then there was a run for the first terrace, when he crouched and listened, then to the next terrace and finally to the wall below the veranda. And then his heart stood still—for as he crouched there, the door from the living room to the veranda closed, and whether it closed on someone going in of course he couldn't tell. But after holding his breath to listen, he decided the coast was clear, and a final dash landed him on the veranda couch with a friendly blanket to cover him."

Such narrow squeaks never deterred Alexander Graham Bell from adopting—indoors or outdoors—"houseboat costume," or from relaxing, as he put it, "in puris naturalibus." The story is told that he was once aroused in this state of nature from slumber on the roof of his houseboat by the loudspeaker of a lake ferry bearing tourists eager for a glimpse of Alexander Graham Bell. Presumably they got more than they bargained for. The ideal summer clothing, he told a *Washington Post* reporter when interviewed about how to beat the heat, is none at all. Perhaps reluctantly, he admitted, "But this our civilization would not permit."

These reminiscences bring to mind the image of a great, brilliant child. Alexander Graham Bell would not have been the least perturbed by such a comparison. He had the greatest respect for children. Freddie Pinaud, whose father, Walter, a noted Nova Scotian designer and builder of yachts who ran Bell's boatyard for many years, says his father used to quote a number of favorite Bell maxims. One of these was: "Always listen to children . . . they might have ideas we've never thought of."

On May 22, 1914, Bell elaborated upon this theme of receptiveness in his speech to the graduating class of the Friends School in Washington, D.C.:

"I was walking one day in my country place in Nova Scotia along the road, when the idea occurred to leave the beaten track and dive into the woods. Well, I had not gone fifty feet before I came upon a gully, and down at the bottom was a beautiful little stream. I never knew of it before.

"Of course, I was not satisfied with the mere discovery, but went down into the gully and explored it right and left. I followed it up to its source. I followed it downwards for half a mile,

The houseboat *Mabel of Beinn Bhreagh,* Bell's favorite retreat. (Charles Martin, 1918)

through a beautiful moss-grown valley, until at last the little stream discharged into a pond, and way in the distance I could see a sea beach with the open water beyond.

"Now just think of that. Here was a beautiful gorge, half a mile long, right on my own place, and coming at one point within fifty feet of a well-trodden road—and I never knew of its existence before! We are all too much inclined, I think, to walk through life with our eyes shut. There are things all around us, and right at our very feet, that we have never seen; because we have never really looked.

"Don't keep forever on the public road, going only where others have gone, and following one after the other like a flock of sheep. Leave the beaten track occasionally and dive into the woods. Every time you do so you will be certain to find something that you have never seen before. Of course it will be a little thing, but do not ignore it. Follow it up, explore all around it; one discovery will lead to another, and before you know it you will have something worth thinking about to occupy your mind. All really big discoveries are the results of thought."

Opposite page:
"We encounter a herd of wild ponies . . . ," Bell wrote on the reverse of this photograph. They were descendants of animals that survived some of the many shipwrecks on Sable Island's shoals.
Left:
The inveterate note-taker at work on Sable Island. (Both, Arthur McCurdy, 1898)

41

For some reason, perhaps because of the romantic movie about their courtship that I had seen in my childhood, a stereotype had also attached itself to the image I had conjured up of Bell's wife, Mabel. It was that of a lucky deaf girl who married and lived happily ever after. But Mabel was always more than lucky. Says Catherine MacDermid, who belongs to the Bell Club, formerly the Young Ladies' Club, which Mabel Bell founded for the young women of the town: "She's just beginning to be noticed; formerly he got all the praise."

Mabel Bell became the American aeronautical industry's first backer, using her own funds as her husband's work progressed

Daisy Bell and Susan McCurdy on Sable Island. (Arthur McCurdy, 1898)

through kites to aircraft in order to support Bell's pioneer think tank and experimental unit, the Aerial Experiment Association (A.E.A.). "I think I understand your experiments," she wrote in January 1895 during the early days of the kite experiments, "even if I don't know the higher mathematics and even if I am not sure whether : : means 'is to' or 'as.' I am sure though that L is to L1 as V1 is to V12—and I think I could explain how you worked out that curve. . . ." Bell knew she could, and in his warm and affectionate letters he sometimes incorporated page upon page of mathematical formulae. And to the end of his life he depended on her avowal, "I believe thoroughly in you, Alec dear."

Mabel was deaf as the result of a childhood illness suffered at the house of her grandfather in New York shortly before her fifth birthday. Her parents, Gertrude McCurdy and Gardiner Greene Hubbard, never accepted the opinions of experts that it was hopeless to expect their daughter to continue to speak. Partially as a re-

"Susie McCurdy in bloomers, riding man fashion," Bell noted on the back of this picture. In the foreground is Daisy and the pony is held by "the oldest inhabitant" of the island. (Arthur McCurdy, 1898)

sult of their efforts, she became a remarkable reader of lips, and in 1867, when she was nine, she stood before a Massachusetts legislative committee and answered questions as her father pressed the house for legislation to provide lip-reading education for all deaf children—today still a controversial option in the education of the deaf.

Mabel had first heard of Alexander Graham Bell when she was at school in Europe and he was a teacher at the Pemberton Avenue School for the Deaf in Boston. Soon after her return to America she went "to see the teacher of whom I had heard so much but whom I privately considered a quack doctor. I both did not and did like him. . . ."

Mabel's feelings quickly became more positive. Her father helped the telephone along with financial and moral support, and she and Alec were married on July 11, 1877, a year after the telephone became a reality. As a wedding present, Bell turned over to his bride 4,990 of the 5,000 shares he received when, two days before the wedding, he, his father-in-law-to-be, and others formed the Bell Telephone Company.

"Mrs. Bell was the one who took everything to heart,"

Arthur McCurdy with the "Ebeddeck," his daylight developing tank, patented in 1906 and given the town's early Indian name.

Mayme told me. "When they had the terrible explosion down in Halifax she and Mother packed all night over at Mother's." Mayme was referring to the collision of the French munitions ship *Mont Blanc* with the Belgian relief ship *Imo* in Halifax Harbour on December 6, 1917, which caused an explosion that devastated the city, killing 1,550 people. She added, "Dr. Bell wouldn't show anything. . . . You'd think he didn't care. But really, he was all right."

Communicating with Mabel did not present many difficulties; in fact, Mayme remembers that sometimes she had the advantage. "Mrs. Bell read your lips. Nobody could fool her. At the silent films she could tell you what everyone on the screen was saying. That was the beautiful part of reading lips! I used to think it was great fun. Once in Washington Mrs. Bell and I were in a streetcar, and a girl and her boyfriend at the back of the car were having a fight. Mrs. Bell said, 'I wish you could hear what that man is telling his girlfriend!' Oh, Mrs. Bell was interested in everything. She went to Dr. Bell's school in Cambridge and fell in love with him . . . but very secretly. She never thought that she would appeal to him. That's the story she told me."

From her notes it is clear how much Daisy Bell Fairchild admired her mother: "Mother always did her own thinking, and it is interesting as I look back and remember about her to realize what a completely original individual she was. I don't think it was just because her deafness saved her from endless objections and criticisms that so many of us hear when we have a new idea to put over. She just knew what she thought would be fun or interesting or worth while to do and then tried to do it. . . .

"One of the guiding forces in my father's life was his devotion to little deaf children . . . His interest in the deaf began when he was hardly more than a lad, and it was deepened by his love for my mother. She was one of the first deaf children in the United States who had been taught to speak and to read the lips and who mingled daily with hearing people . . . Knowing her, he knew it was possible for someone totally deaf from early childhood to be an outstanding individual in a hearing world."

The Bells had four children: their daughters, Elsie May and Daisy, and then two sons, whose deaths very shortly after their births Mabel called "almost my deepest sorrow." Like all children, Daisy and her elder sister, Elsie May, "took things as we found them for granted." They knew their father had invented the telephone, but when the twelve-year-old Daisy was at boarding school and one of the girls asked if the telephone was called the Bell telephone after her father or because you rang a bell to call Central, Daisy said she didn't know.

All the same, they were a scientist's offspring. Elsie May reported that when they were very small and went out for walks, they used to play "atoms," ricocheting off each other back and forth across the sidewalk.

Mayme Morrison Brown knew the Bell daughters well. "The two girls were somewhat older than I. They were great fun. Daisy Fairchild was a bushel of fun. Any tricks or deviltry Daisy got up to, that was all right with Dr. Bell.

"They used to ride horseback—sidesaddle—and there was a fellow, definitely English, who had a crush on Daisy. They used to take him horseback riding. I still remember the gray suit he wore and the hat and the white shirt with the starched front. Well, Daisy thought she'd have some fun one day and she rode around to where there was a culvert and below that a bog. Daisy's horse was well acquainted with it, and she jumped it easily; he came right behind and went into the bog. He was splashed all over; he decided then he'd better leave!

"Dr. Bell knew right away. He said, 'Daisy did that from devilment.' He was getting a kick out of it. But Mrs. Bell was cross. She knew it was a trick and she thought it was terrible. But she used to say, 'That finished him.' Daisy was full of the dickens.

"Elsie Grosvenor was somewhat quieter. She had been rather sickly as a child, and when she was about fifteen or sixteen she had a bad scare. She was out on the mountain on horseback entirely away from the highway, and the horse threw her. They couldn't find her for two or three days. They were all searching. They were nearly crazy with worry. My uncle Don found her. It was at night and a storm was coming up and he had taken a lantern and was following along a brook that led out of his pasture looking for a horse. He went by a cave in the bank and heard whimpering. She'd got lost and gone into the cave. She grabbed hold of his neck and wouldn't let go, so he carried her home to his house and gave her a scoop of honey and some warm milk. That brought her out of it.

"She was married in England in 1901 to Dr. Gilbert Grosvenor, the editor of the *National Geographic.* I remember being a little girl down at the reception they had when they came home. All the trees were lit up with Japanese lanterns. Everybody was there."

During the Bells' early days in Nova Scotia, an important member of their circle was Arthur McCurdy, who became Bell's secretary and assistant in 1886. The Bell-McCurdy association proved to be a close and eventful one. Perhaps particularly after their father was widowed, the McCurdy children—Susan, George,

Beinn Bhreagh Hall, completed in
1893. Directly above the main
porch is Bell's sleeping porch.
(Notman Studios, 1912–1916)

Douglas, and Lucien—became part of an extended family, with the boys standing by to take photographs, fly on a kite, or design and fly an aircraft. Susan's name often crops up when Bell's notes and letters touch on domestic matters. "Did anyone tell you of the *awful* time we had last week with Susie McCurdy?" he wrote Mabel when Daisy, an art student, tried to take a plaster cast of Susie's face and then could not get the plaster off. "How long they had been working over it before I was called I do not know, but when I arrived on the scene there was Susie, on her back on a sofa—helpless—with a mass of plaster weighing several pounds completely covering her face and apparently as hard as stone . . ." Susie's brother George brought a meat saw, and the operation of removing the mask continued for "about five and a half hours." Bell sent Susie flowers when she made her debut and named the *Frost King,* one of his most important kites, in honor of her marriage to Walter (Jack) Frost in 1905.

Somehow the McCurdys "claimed relationship with the Bells . . . through Mrs. Bell's mother's family. I could never figure it out,"* Mayme told me. The story of Bell's first encounter in Baddeck with McCurdy is well known. Mayme relates that "Arthur McCurdy had a newspaper and an office down the Baddeck wharf and when Dr. Bell was first here, McCurdy didn't know who he was. He had a telephone that was out of order. Dr. Bell picked it up and found a fly in the transmitter. It interfered with the voice. But McCurdy said, 'You mustn't do that. I don't allow anyone to use my phones!' Dr. Bell used to laugh about it . . . and how he began telling him about the inventor!"

The telephone in question was part of Nova Scotia's first hookup—a private line linking the McCurdy family businesses. Advertisements for "cheap and instantaneous communication by direct sound" through "the speaking telephone of Alexander Graham Bell" were everywhere at the time. "It needs no batteries, has no moving machinery, and no skill is required. Only talk as if in ordinary conversation—and listen attentively."

Daisy's notes indicate how much Arthur McCurdy meant to the Bells. "Mr. McCurdy came into our lives then and was intimately associated with us for twenty years. He was full of energy and initiative, loved doing out-of-door things and carried out Father and Mother's ideas with enthusiasm. . . .

"He gave both Mother and Father a kind of *young* friendship that they never had with anyone else. They had jolly carefree

---

* A possible distant relationship is suggested in *The McCurdys of Nova Scotia,* edited and compiled by H. Percy Blanchard and published in 1930 for the Hon. F. B. McCurdy, Halifax, Nova Scotia, by the Covenant Publishing Company, London, England.

times with him out of doors cutting trails through the woods, exploring the water's edge in a canoe or climbing up waterfalls, out on showshoes in the wintertime. He was an expert at it all and they were not, and they did things with him that they could never have done without him. This was especially true, of course, of Mother, who was so terribly handicapped by her lack of balance."

The family sometimes went to a get-away cabin they had built in the Cape Breton woods. Other excursions took them surprisingly far afield—on one occasion to Sable Island, the so-called graveyard of the Atlantic. The purpose of this trip was to look for wreckage of a ship in which friends had lost their lives, and to find a pony for Daisy. (The island is still today home to herds of wild ponies, descendants of those shipwrecked on the island's shoals.) As usual, McCurdy was photographer to the expedition. "I start off with Supt. Boutilier [the lighthouse keeper] to patrol the shore of the island in search of bodies or wreckage . . . ," Bell wrote on one print from this excursion, a photograph showing him driving through the surf in a carriage.

While working for Bell, Arthur McCurdy became an inventor himself. He developed a handy daylight developing tank and sold the rights to Eastman Kodak. In 1902 he remarried, his second wife being a niece of Bell's new stepmother (Bell's mother had died in 1897). A daughter by this marriage, Leonora McCurdy Towell of Vancouver, British Columbia, recalling the tank, said, "The film had to be in the dark, but not Father. If Mr. Bell wanted photographs of his kites or anything, he said to my father, 'You're the photographer.' "

Beverly Brannan, curator of the photographic collections in the Prints and Photographs Division of the Library of Congress, writing in an article on the Gilbert H. Grosvenor Collection of Alexander Graham Bell Photographs, notes that Bell had learned to take pictures and develop the prints as a boy from his father, when photography was still in its infancy. He was an early enthusiast of the camera's incomparable documentary power, and McCurdy was the first of a line of employees Bell had photograph and record his experiments and activities.

Eventually McCurdy moved with his second family to Victoria, British Columbia, where he continued "snapshotting" and developing until his death in 1923. But perhaps McCurdy caught his most evocative image on Sable Island in 1898: Alexander and Mabel Bell, their backs to the camera, hand-in-hand, viewing the distance. Bell wrote on the print, "Mabel and I think ourselves alone but photographer McCurdy steals up behind us and secures a snapshot."

The expenditure of what the press called "American gold"—twenty-two thousand dollars—had made Bell's Beinn Bhreagh Hall, generally known as the Point House, the biggest, grandest house in Cape Breton. It was radically different from the Lodge, the rustic summer residence the Bells had constructed as a stopgap on their headland property, and a far cry indeed from Crescent Grove, where the family made their own furniture by stuffing mattresses with straw and the children learned to churn butter while

Four generations in a photograph taken shortly after the birth of the Bells' first grandchild. Melville Grosvenor is in the lap of his mother, Elsie Bell Grosvenor, with Alexander Graham Bell looking on. Alexander Melville Bell is seated beside Elsie. (Bachrach, 1901)

The library at Beinn Bhreagh
Hall.

The living room, with its huge fireplace. (David Fairchild, 1922)

A vine-clad arbor on the estate.
(Notman Studios, 1912–1916)

52

Bell played "Onward, Christian Soldiers" as encouragement. The Point House squats above the red cliffs, turreted, rambling, Victorian. "I didn't know it was an ugly house until we grew up and one of my sisters went to art school," Bell's granddaughter Lilian Grosvenor Jones wrote in *The New Yorker*.

Eventually miles of road crossed the mountaintop and wharves, workshops, the staff house, and Bell's laboratory all were built. There was a farm—"Dr. Bell liked his own eggs and his own butter," Mayme Morrison Brown remembers—and a large staff. There were orchards and gardens. "He always praised it up, if it was good," remembers Tom Roberts, once one of the Beinn Bhreagh gardeners.

Mabel Bell handled the family finances and ran the estate. Sometimes in private letters she lamented the cost in "good dollars" of all the maintenance and construction. But Beinn Bhreagh was always a pleasure. "The lake is like a vast white plain," she wrote in her later life to son-in-law Bert Grosvenor, "from which the hills rise and there are leafless trees forming the foreground, their branches forming delicate tracery against the white background. And the great lake plain is never the same five minutes at a time. There is such constant play of light and shade and blue and purple and all the wonderful golden colours of the sunset. I not only have the sunset but also the sunrise, it comes in one window in the morning and the sunset in another, all in the same charmed room. And the moon—there is nothing like its glory elsewhere. I am not so sure but I love Beinn Bhreagh winters even better than its summers. . . ."

The Beinn Bhreagh life-style fascinated all. "They always had a crowd at their place," remembers Mayme Morrison Brown. "All the family used to come." The roster included Mabel's parents, her sisters and their families, Alec's parents (and later his stepmother), his sister-in-law—the widow of one of his two brothers—and a large assortment of cousins and connections. And in the new century there were sons-in-law and grandchildren.

"They were building the Point House when I was born," says Mayme. "Two men from Truro were staying with Mother doing the mason work. I know every crick and corner. To some people it was a spooky house, but I never found it so. It's all ghosts in Cape Breton. The old people really believed in them. The stories I've heard—they get better as the evening goes on. They used to say there was a ghost over at Beinn Bhreagh—a headless woman. They said the Hubbards, Mrs. Bell's family, murdered a person way back and that that was how they got their money; Dr. Bell didn't have any money.* The doors would creak and open by

* Until he invented the telephone.

themselves. Some people thought they saw the ghost. But I think if there's a ghost there, it's Dr. Bell's!

"Some woman told me she's heard there were a hundred rooms in the house. I said, 'Good heavens, no. Eleven fireplaces, though.' "

One of these fireplaces was the responsibility, during a summer vacation, of seventeen-year-old Dan Stewart, whose father, William, spent most of his working days at Beinn Bhreagh as chief carpenter. "My father had lots of influence to get me something to do, so I was employed as sort of caretaker. Around six in the morning I was supposed to go directly to Dr. Bell's study and start up a fire in the fireplace so he'd have it when he woke up. He slept in a great big open porch facing the driveway in what you might call a two-story bed. Homemade.

"We didn't have a fireplace at home, and for a few days I did something like I'd do on the kitchen range: a bunch of paper and a few kindlings on top, strike a match, and let it go. It wasn't long before Dr. Bell asked me to come and see him in the morning. He said, 'I see you're not familiar with lighting a fire in a fireplace and I'm going to give you some instructions.' We both knelt down at the fireplace and he showed me how to put the papers under and put the kindling crisscross, the second tier at right angles to the first and so on. After that, a couple of harder sticks on top. That way the fire would have a chance to circulate through the openings and flare up and catch quicker and I'd get through that part of my work quicker. How interesting he made it for me . . . and how pleasant."

Mayme explained that "Dr. and Mrs. Bell always slept in Dr. Bell's porch. He had it built outside his study and he had a four-poster built from rough pine. He used to have every issue of the *National Geographic* stashed up there, and Daisy Fairchild said if you touched one he knew it. They always slept out there—both of them. But many's the night he just didn't want to go to bed, he wanted to study. One night he evidently didn't want to sleep out there, and it was a very cold night. Mrs. Bell had those geneva gin jars—they were long and narrow crockery jars and they were great to put hot water in and warm the bed. She had two of them—they made great foot warmers. You put in a good big cork and a cap over it to stop them from leaking. Dr. Bell got into bed and punched a hole in one of them so that by and by the whole bed was soaking wet and they had to come into the bedroom. He wondered how it happened!

"In the morning he wouldn't open his eyes till he had a hot towel over them. He had lovely black eyes . . . the most expressive eyes. He had to have a hot towel . . . house temperature . . . over

The porch, with a telescope at the right. (Notman Studios, 1912–1916)

his eyes before the light would strike them. If he didn't have that towel he might scare the daylights out of you. There was a girl working there—she came from Washington with them—and she was very nervous. The least little thing.... So one day she went to wake him with her hot towel. But he was awake; he jumped up. He jumped up and she took off!"

Getting Alexander Graham Bell up in the morning was not for the faint-hearted. First responsibility rested with Charles Thompson, his articulate black butler: "The seriousness, to me, in getting Mr. Bell up in time for any important engagement was that if I did not succeed in getting him up, he placed the entire responsibility on me." When faced with a hopeless situation he would summon Mrs. Bell and "if Mrs. Bell was in the house we very seldom ever failed."

Elsie May, the elder daughter, was not so lucky, and in the notes that she, like Daisy and Charles the butler wrote after her parents' deaths, she discussed the complexity of the task. "It was practically impossible to wake him until he had had his sleep out. He used to say that if he was working on a particularly difficult and intricate problem he would get it clearly in his mind before going to sleep and would find it solved subconsciously when he woke in the morning. He was so hard to awaken that he often stayed up all night in order to be up on time for an early morning engagement. His eyes were very sensitive to light and he used to wind a heavy bath towel around his head to keep out the light. When first awakened if his shades were raised too suddenly it would give him a violent headache and render him useless for the day!"

And Bell himself wrote to Mabel (on September 2, 1906): "We all returned yesterday from Sydney on the steamer *Beverly*. I stayed up all night Saturday so as to catch the boat in the morning without difficulty and lay down in a stateroom the moment I got on board. I slept all the way to Baddeck and then Elsie made

Alexander Melville Bell with his second wife, Harriet (holding Melville Grosvenor), and Elsie Bell Grosvenor on the porch at Beinn Bhreagh, 1902.

an awful mistake in trying to arouse me. She tried to pull off my eye-bandage and succeeded in letting a flood of light fall on my darkened eyes. I woke at once with the pain in my eyes but did not understand quite where I was. I thought I was in Sydney and she was trying to get me up for the boat. She did not explain but tugged away at my eye-bandage with all her strength. Aroused in this rough manner I said I would not get up—they might go without me—and I would follow by the next train. Still she did not explain but poured a glass full of water over me—clothes and all—I had not undressed . . . After a while, as I was soaked, I got up intending to change my things—and found to my surprise that I was on board the *Beverly* at the wharf in Baddeck."

Once up, Alexander Graham Bell liked a good breakfast, but he did not necessarily get his own way. Beginning shortly after his marriage Bell battled problems of overweight, writing once to Mabel that he had achieved 208 pounds—"quite a come-down." Mabel encouraged reduction by exercise and diet, but it was a battle never won.

Mayme recalls that "Mrs. Bell was trying to keep him on a diet just because he was putting on too much poundage. He was supposed to have sugar . . . diabetes . . . he wasn't a bit careful. For years I don't think they knew he had it, but in the last years they did discover. Once I took his tray up in the morning and put it on his desk. I uncovered his dish . . . it was cereal . . . dry cereal! Mrs. Bell ordered that.

"Well, he got wild. He said, 'A grand old Scotsman sitting here and cannot get his porridge!' He was wild; he couldn't get his porridge. Then I uncovered a jar of cream cheese . . . there were skippers on the top of it. 'Dr. Bell,' I said, 'it's got wormy.' But he said, 'Come here, Mayme. Sit down.' He took his knife and ran it over the cheese top. 'That's bacteria . . . that's the healthiest kind of cheese.' He explained the whole thing. 'That's just bacteria crawling around!' All the skippers on the top . . . he mashed them up and put them on his toast!

"That was the lovely part of Dr. Bell. He never thought he was wasting time. He'd explain the whole thing to you if you asked him questions."

Animals, too, are part of the legend. There was a horse with cart attached that backed up to a cliff, fell over, and walked home along the beach, cart and all. There was also Bell's favorite white riding horse; he'd stop whenever Bell wanted him to and wait. According to Daisy, her father loved "any and all" animals; her mother loved them less. "But Father didn't love them enough to take any responsibility about them and he always knew that Mother would."

Mayme told me: "Dr. Bell had his own menagerie. Just his own collection—not large—but he had bobcats and a wild cat with a long tail. And he had white-headed eagles—four of them at one time. He let them go but they stayed around. There was an old tree below the Point House and two of them were always there. You know, an eagle lives to quite an old age—over a hundred. Dr. Bell loved them. He was observing them, trying to learn their habits.

"And he was interested in some breed of snake that was here in Red Head. One day I saw one of the kind he was talking about. My sister Marguerite and I were out picking turnips or veg. She was sitting on a pile of rocks and this one appeared—all colors and spots on it. I pinched my sister's arm and beckoned her away over the field. Next time I saw Dr. Bell I told him about it, and he had the men look everywhere around our fields. Mother said it was there in the rocks all summer. But I think the boys were afraid to find it. Well, let's face it, it was a *snake*!

"Dr. Bell also had a bear. He bought it when it was young from a trapper that used to go around trapping wild animals for circuses. They had it in a cage and it grew quite big. They had the animals down near the warehouse, and one day I went in with some message for Mr. Byrnes, the estate superintendent. I heard scratching between the office and the cage. I said, 'I think Bruno is trying to work his way through!' Well, he had the whole wall chewed through. Mr. Byrnes said, 'We'll have to get rid of him because if he gets loose among people he knows so well nothing will scare him.'

"So they had him stuffed. He was there for the longest time on the front veranda. He used to scare a lot of people—his teeth were showing.

"Dr. Bell's butler was Charles Thompson, and there was a second man, too, called Louis Hill. He was a mulatto, and he was always playing tricks. He used to go down to Fairchilds' to call on a Swedish girl there. Charles was full of mischief, too, and one evening I said, 'I'll tell you what we'll do, Charles; we'll call him and tell him Mrs. Bell got a call from Baddeck and unexpectedly has a lot of company coming for dinner at seven-thirty and he'd better get over.' Well, poor Louis was mad but he started out. It was a long distance between the Fairchilds' and the Point House, and dark in the evenings. We took the bear down, and put it in the middle of the road. I'd been telling them at the dinner table about the wild animals of Cape Breton. I'd been saying that if a bear was standing up and he caught you he'd hug you and squeeze you to death!

"Poor Louis came running and he ran right into the bear in

Above:
Melville in his grandfather's arms. Also out for the ride are his great-grandfather Alexander Melville Bell, Harriet Bell, and mother Elsie Bell Grosvenor.
Left:
Champ receives a lump of sugar. (Both, Gilbert Grosvenor, 1902–1903)

Melville Grosvenor playing "horsey" with Grandfather while Champ waits patiently. (Gilbert Grosvenor, 1909)

the middle of the road in the dark. Scared! . . . He took off round the garden. In the meantime we put the bear back. We didn't have far to move it.

" 'Thank God I got home,' he said.

"We didn't dare to tell him!

"Well, they weren't looking after that bear too well, and it got mothy and the hair came out. So they got another one, but not as nice as the first."

Opinion varies in Baddeck as to whether Bell sometimes gave vent to a hot temper, or invariably displayed a serene, even saintly, countenance. Officially the balance is tipped toward the saintly side of the scale. One or two of the stories I heard from official sources bore a striking similarity to those told of Queen Victoria.

In his lifetime, particularly in his early years in Baddeck, there was speculation as to Bell's mental health, and some gossip. Catherine MacKenzie, Bell's last secretary, wrote that he once threatened to call a policeman into his house to confront an employee who indulged in talk.

Did Bell's eye ever wander (some of the old people say it did) when, after the death of their infant sons, he and Mabel practiced the strictest birth control? Their letters show them caught in a predicament of the time. Bell feared pregnancy for Mabel ("I love you too much to risk your life"), and so he counseled abstinence and holidays without him.

Mabel Bell herself never claimed perfection in her husband. "I do not know a person he has not fought with some time or other, and sometimes I, his wife, have thought him badly in the wrong, and at others entirely in the right," she wrote when discussing the question of an eventual biography shortly before Bell's death. It was not, she insisted, to be written by a member of the family; she disliked the idea of eulogistic treatment for her husband because he was, she stoutly contended, "big enough to stand as he is."

Like most of us, Bell impressed different people differently. Freddie Pinaud and his wife, Henrietta, both come of families who knew Bell well. "My father thought the world of him," Freddie Pinaud remembers. "I knew some of the people who thought there was something wrong with him . . . that he was on the verge . . . kites, planes . . . there was no sense in them. God, it hurt my father terrifically to think anybody would suggest that. But my wife's mother worked for him, and I think he had quite a temper, although my father never told me. If things weren't going right it would flare up."

Henrietta Pinaud, whose mother, Georgina Haliburton MacLeod, was for many years Mabel Bell's personal maid, says, "My mother wasn't particularly fond of Dr. Bell. She loved Mrs. Bell. One evening Dr. Bell came from his little place at the back of Red Head where he used to do his writing and Mrs. Bell told somebody to tell him there was going to be company she wanted him to meet, but he wasn't in the mood for company. Mrs. Bell told my mother, 'Georgie, help Mr. Bell get dressed.' Of course, the shirts then weren't open all the way down the front and they had the studs, you know. Well, I don't know what he found wrong with the first shirt . . . oh, he was in a bad mood, that was it . . . and he found the shirt too tight or something . . . he didn't like dressing . . . he didn't want the bother. And he said, 'Take this thing and take it somewhere I'll never see it as long as I live!' My mother had a pretty good temper herself, and she just took it and tore it and pulled it right off him. Then she took out another shirt, and she had gotten so nervous and angry that the stud fell down inside. 'Now,' he said, 'what do you expect to do about that?' She said, 'Don't worry!' and she took a little pair of scissors out of her pocket and snipped a little hole and pulled it out! That night when Mrs. Bell was going to bed and my mother was combing her hair, Mrs. Bell looked in the mirror and saw my mother looking so tired! 'Oh,' she said. 'You poor child! Alec was telling me what fun he had with you!' Oh, trying! Mrs. Bell had such patience with him."

Mayme agrees. "He could be cranky—just for a minute. But he made up for it later. He'd come back and he'd be all smiles and as sweet as could be. Mrs. Bell was wonderful with him. 'Don't pay any attention to Alec,' she'd say. She'd say it on the sly.

"You didn't know what he'd do next. He once took one of Mrs. Bell's venetian blinds for one of his experiments. Anything he wanted, he'd take it. Oh, yes, sometimes she'd get cross. She could. But then he'd go over and put his hand on hers and say, 'My dear,' and it would all be over."

Life with a genius father required flexibility but, according to Daisy, was always harmonious. "Things always went smoothly at home. I can't find as I look back over my childhood and youth any unpleasant or critical memories or impressions of anyone. Father and Mother only looked for the best in people—and Father wouldn't tolerate the least disparagement of anyone. As we girls grew older we wanted to talk people over and we wanted to gossip and we wanted to criticise, but we never could do it before Father. If we began it at table, Father would become absolutely silent. He never even criticised us for doing it, but he would look more and more disapproving, and sometimes push back his chair, put his napkin on the table and prepare to leave, but I don't think we ever actually drove him to that.

"I don't think Elsie and I were ever ultra-disagreeable about people, but we couldn't even criticise officials in public life, and worst of all sins was to 'impute motives' to other people. Just try to talk politics without doing that!

"And you can imagine the difficulties in dismissing an employee—'the boys' [his associates in the Aerial Experiment Association] were later to find that out—for Father always stood up for the person 'abused' or 'accused.' "

But the analytical mind was always there. In 1901 brigands near the frontier line of Bulgaria and Turkey captured an American woman missionary and demanded a ransom of $100,000 for her release, an incident that culminated in a confrontation be-

Bell and his grandson cross a bridge. (About 1908)

tween the brigands and Theodore Roosevelt and many years later inspired the 1975 movie *The Wind and the Lion.* In response to a telegram soliciting his aid—MISS STONE DIES TOMORROW . . . LIFE OR DEATH . . . PLEASE WIRE HELP—Bell ruminated in his notes on personal as opposed to civic loyalty and penned a comment on terrorism:

"What a prize Mabel would be should she return to Sicily, et cetera, et cetera. . . . The thought occurs, what would I do if Mabel should be captured and held for ransom? Well, there then comes a conflict between my duty as an individual and my duty as a citizen of the United States. I would then find out whether I am more of a citizen than a man—or more of a man than a citizen. Whatever my individual action might be I would still hold that the GENERAL good demanded that the ransom should not be paid—whether I should pay it myself is quite another thing.

"$100,000 is quite a large sum. Surely the GENERAL GOOD would be more advanced to use it to effect the capture and punishment of the brigands than to reward them. As I am not a relative of Miss Stone, or personally interested in her, the CITIZEN outweighs the man in her case."

Exploring Right and Left

Alexander Graham Bell kept regular hours—even if they seemed irregular to others. Daisy reports that he had a deep feeling about having the right atmosphere in which to think; he trained himself so that his physical surroundings induced specific trains of thought. "In the little office near the laboratory he occupied his mind with problems connected with the experiments then going on—in his study in the house he thought and worked over his theories of gravitation and so on—while the *Mabel of Beinn Bhreagh* was the place to think of genetics and heredity."

His involvement in his work often set Bell apart both physically and mentally and sometimes occasioned letters from Mabel with the query, "I wonder do you ever think of me in the midst of that work of yours of which I am so proud and yet so jealous. . . ." He was often contrite but did not reform. "My deaf mute researches have taken me away—far away—from you all," he wrote ten years after their marriage while undertaking an important statistical study. "I don't think your thoughts—or feel your feelings—nothing but deaf-mute—deaf-mute—and solitude in my mind. . . . While my thoughts run in the deaf-mute line I am practically vanished from the family."

Notebook jottings show that Bell foresaw discoveries and inventions later made by others. His theorizing brought him close at various times to television as well as to the tape recorder, and some of his provocative thoughts—those on solar heat, for instance—foreshadow preoccupations of our own day. Many seminal thoughts Bell never followed up, but other ideas became projects on which he worked intermittently over decades.

Bell's weekends on the houseboat were an important feature of his summers. Mayme Morrison Brown tells of visiting him there when he was working on the problem of "the dial phone." It is generally thought that Bell did no work on the automatic switchboard after 1897; and, in fact, the automatic switchboard was invented by others the first installation taking place in Laporte, Indiana, in 1892. However, improvements, many of them major, were to take place across the United States and Canada over the

Opposite page:
Bell with granddaughters Gertrude (left), Lilian (held), and Mabel Grosvenor. (Gilbert Grosvenor, 1909)

Opposite page:
Daisy Bell Fairchild on the after-
deck of the *Mabel of Beinn Bhreagh*.
(David Fairchild, 1922–1923)

next decades and even into the twenties and thirties. Well after the turn of the century Bell apparently thought there was still much work to be done.

"I used to go down to the floating palace to take him his lunch," Mayme explained. "But he wanted a lot more to eat than that. So I was cooking him hard-boiled eggs on the sly. I used to go up to the gardener's place, and I'd boil him a dozen the way he liked them . . . weedy, more like they were coddled, but still in the shell. I said to him one day, 'Dr. Bell, why do you eat so many eggs?' He answered, 'They're the only thing in here the flies won't shit on!' He told me in plain English! Well, that word is in the Bible—several times! He laughed so hard his whiskers shook. He'd crack an egg and eat it while he worked. He loved to get down to the floating palace so he could eat as much as he wanted. He used to go down to work. He experimented with the dial phone there. That was 1911 or 1912, in the fall. He was getting old then.

"I remember the Sunday he struck it. He had tested and worked all night, and he'd gone in swimming without his clothes. That was nothing for him! He heard the carriage coming, and he yelled out to John MacDermid, was I with him? John said yes, and he said, 'Stay back.' He'd got on his bathrobe by the time we arrived.

"He said, 'Come here and sit down.' He had chained little flashlight bulbs all around a little wall and in front he had a seat. They were just ordinary flashlight bulbs in different colors—white and green and yellow and red. They were very tiny, and there must have been nine or ten. He pressed a little button and they all lit. He'd been able to get one or two for a long time; he'd been shifting things around. 'I've got it! I've got it!' he said. He was as happy as if somebody had given him a medal. When he had something he was working on, he stuck with it until he won it.

"I remember distinctly when I saw all the lights come on I asked him if he was going to patent it. He stopped to think and with a frown on he said he didn't know. He said, 'It will put so many out of work. Right in Washington alone it would put eight hundred girls out of work.' Work at that time wasn't too brisk either, and Dr. Bell didn't like to see anybody out of work.

"Well, I'm quite sure that somebody did patent it, even if he didn't."

Despite the automatic switchboard, or perhaps because of it, the Telephone Pioneers of America, founded in 1911 by veteran telephone employees, today numbers about half a million members in the United States and Canada, making this service organization of men and women who have spent their working lives in the industry the largest organization of its kind in the world.

Members give hours of service to the blind, the deaf, and the handicapped. Recently the Pioneers developed a sound-equipped ball, strong enough to keep on beeping after being hit with a bat, for blind children who like to play baseball.

Bell's interest in the education of the deaf was a mainspring of his life. "I shall never leave this work," he vowed in a letter to Mabel on November 22, 1876, when the telephone was just beginning to make him famous. He was the third generation of his family—his grandfather, first an actor, later became a teacher of elocution—to study the voice and its projection. While he was still in his teens, his father developed what had been internationally sought, a universally applicable phonetic alphabet, and Bell and his brothers helped demonstrate its usefulness. It was as a teacher of his father's system of Visible Speech that he originally went to Boston. After the invention of the telephone, he fulfilled a dream and opened his own school for the deaf in Washington, D.C., which he operated until pressure of litigation over his telephone patents forced him to close it. He remained an authority in the field and throughout his life devoted study, time, and money to the cause of the deaf.

At Beinn Bhreagh, Bell once showed Mayme Morrison a human ear he kept handy. Mayme told me, "That's how he experimented on the eardrum. He said scientists had them for medical research. I was only a very little girl, and I remember how scared I was!"

For deaf and blind Helen Keller—brought to him when she was six years old by her father, who sought his advice—Bell had special affection. He helped find Helen's remarkable teacher, Anne Sullivan Macy, and followed their progress with paternal pride. The biographer Joseph P. Lash recounts in *Helen and Teacher* a conversation Bell had with Helen that illustrates the prior claim the deaf always had on his attention. "One would think I had never done anything worthwhile but the telephone," he spelled into Helen's hand. "That is because it is a money-making invention. It is a pity so many people make money the criterion of success. I wish my experiences had resulted in enabling the deaf to speak with less difficulty. That would have made me truly happy." Helen dedicated her autobiography *The Story of My Life* "to Alexander Graham Bell who taught the deaf to speak . . ." She made a number of visits to Beinn Bhreagh, one of them in August 1901, when she was twenty years old.

Mayme Morrison Brown recalls the occasion: "I remember the deaf and blind girl Helen Keller giving me a prize for sack racing. Every August Dr. Bell put on a gala time—'harvest home.' They'd invite all the people of Victoria County. They'd have

71

everything to entertain the people. Bag races—you'd get in a bag and race—potato races. Running and jumping like in the Olympics. Catching the greased pig—a pig all greased up with the axle grease of the wagons. Helen Keller gave all the prizes away that night in the warehouse . . . a very nice-looking woman. She'd put her fingers on your lips. She'd know everything you said to her. Her voice wasn't a whisper . . . just kind of a gurgle in her throat. She stayed for the dance . . . till about three or four in the morning. John MacDermid took her dancing. . . . He was the coachman."

Newspaper accounts of the time report that Helen said "something appropriate" to the prizewinners, and remembered all their names. She also participated in kite experiments that Bell always had in progress. "I helped him fly some kites and was almost carried up by one," she told a Boston *Transcript* reporter. Helen did bead work and was able to tell by feel whether a kite's wire strings would hold or not. "One day I said to Dr. Bell, 'Won't this string break?' 'Oh, no,' he said, confidently; but in a few moments my fears were realized . . . the string snapped and off went the kite, and poor Dr. Bell stood forlornly looking after it."

Bell's sheep-breeding experiments were the most long-continued of all the Beinn Bhreagh projects. In 1890 Bell began breeding the flock that came with the parcel of land he had bought from Donald McAulay, Mayme's relative. Sheep have only one pair of functioning nipples, although often there are additional rudimentary sets; Bell now tried to discover if multiple births were somehow related to the number of these nipples. Actually, he had become interested in the subject of reproduction and breeding almost as soon as he came to Baddeck. The first year the Bells summered on Crescent Grove he gave his daughters a pet lamb. When the family returned the next year, the lamb was already a mother. "But why only one lamb?" wrote Mabel when she recalled the origins of the experiments many years later. "Would not twins double the farmer's income without materially increasing his labour?

"The argument that he preferred one good lamb to two poor ones did not seem conclusive to Mr. Bell for the farmer most certainly had no objection to many pig babies, and neither the pig nor the dog mother had difficulty in rearing a large proportion of their children to fine maturity. Why could not the sheep do so too? The problem fascinated Mr. Bell. Here was what seemed to him an opportunity to satisfy his scientific curiosity, and at the same time serve the people among whom he had made his home."

Bell first housed his sheep on top of the mountain and constructed a sheep village—he called it Sheepville—with pens built to his own specifications, along with a photographic dark room. (Arthur McCurdy began his photographic career at this time, taking lessons from a Mr. Watson in Baddeck in order to photograph the sheep families.) Early in April 1891 Bell rushed back from Washington, D.C., for his first lambing season. He climbed the mountain, spent a night bedded down under a table in the shepherds' hut—quarters he shared with the three "boys" who looked after the flock (they had the bed) and with three motherless lambs—and then erected a tent and passed most of the month camping out. He found twins and extra nipples abounding. In a letter datelined "Sheepville," he wrote Mabel, "One of the extra nippled Ewes gives milk *from all four nipples*—promising."

Helen Keller with Bell, 1901.

73

Lauchie E. MacDonald, for forty years high sheriff in Baddeck, until recently worked four or five shifts a week as commissionaire at the Alexander Graham Bell National Historic Park "answering questions visitors ask." In 1910, when Lauchie was seventeen and "looking for to make a dollar," he worked in the sheep shed at Beinn Bhreagh:

"Dr. Bell had this flock of sheep, and he found a female with four nipples instead of two. And he found a male the same, and he crossed them and he got six nipples and twins. He crossed them again and got eight nipples and triplets.

"He had about half a dozen eight-nipple rams, and he used to give them out to the farmers to breed their flock. If you struck an eight-nipple lamb he gave you ten dollars where the butcher only paid three. He thought he was going to get them to have nipples all up their underparts and have litters like pigs or pups.

"We had a farm and we had a flock of beautiful purebred sheep, and my father got those rams for three or four winters and we got three or four of those ten-dollar lambs.

"But we ended up with a flock of scrubs. You see, Dr. Bell didn't care what breed his sheep were so long as they had the nipples!

"And there was another thing: he had something like a big boxing glove set up for the rams to bump their heads on. If they took to it, he was going to get an instrument to measure the hits because the one that hit hardest he was going to use for breeding.

"But they didn't take to it."

Bell kept meticulous records on his many-nippled sheep, devising his own method of identification, and the breeding experiments continued under various auspices until 1941, when the United States Department of Agriculture decided that "the multi-nipple character has no practical value in sheep production." However, to some the matter remains open to question. Although "200 percent lambing"—twinning—is still the objective of the American Sheep Improvement Association, through better understanding of nutrition, genetics, and physiology it is now possible to breed prolific sheep that regularly birth four or more lambs. But they still have only two nipples, and according to Professor H. Garino of the animal science department of the MacDonald Campus of McGill University, the offspring frequently have to be artificially fed. Additional functioning nipples and milk bags would certainly be an advantage.

The death of Bell's infant son from breathing difficulties in 1881 inspired him to have an apparatus made up in England that would serve the same purpose as the modern iron lung—that of maintaining artificial respiration. Bell made tests with a number of vacuum jackets over a number of years. The last test recorded in his notes describes the occasion when "an apparatus for producing artificial respiration was tried by Miss Marian Hubbard Bell." This occurred in 1898 after Daisy drew sketches for an artificial respiration device in her father's laboratory notes. For Daisy's experiment, Bell decided to revive a drowned sheep—he had previously conducted some experiments with cats—and he personally selected a young ram from his flock. The animal won a reprieve when six nipples were counted. The test was rescheduled and took place several days later with another animal after lots were drawn to determine who should dispatch the sheep. The task fell to Bell, who pasted into his laboratory notes for September 3, 1898, a tab of paper on which Daisy had identified the unfortunate winner of the lottery as "the man who is willing to do what he doesn't want to do for the sake of saving human lives." On this occasion the sheep died—because, Bell believed, it took an hour to get the vacuum jacket working.

Helen Keller and Alexander Bell kite-flying in a Beinn Bhreagh meadow, 1901. "I helped him fly some kites and was almost carried up by one," she told a Boston journalist.

Helen Keller and Alexander Bell.

Mayme Morrison Brown remembers a later successful test: "The iron lung in the hospitals today is really from Dr. Bell's experiments. I was out in the boat with him and a bunch of us and John Davison, the old shepherd, the day he half-drowned a sheep. I was quite young—nine or ten. They threw her over and weighted her down and kept her under the water by hand. It doesn't take much to drown a sheep.

"If you let go, the wool is so heavy they'll go right to the bottom. I'd say she was about dead when they took the vacuum out of the back seat and pumped the water out of her lungs. Oh, the sheep survived. Absolutely!

"That experiment upset some people. They didn't know what he was doing. They thought he had some kind of magic hand. I think they thought he was working black magic . . . the devil possessed it anyway. A lot of the old people thought this; they wouldn't leave their jobs but they were nervy."

Other lines of experimental research Bell followed up for many years involved condensation of water from the atmosphere and desalination. He was still refining these ideas in 1919. "He was trying to benefit sailors when they were shipwrecked," Mayme remembers. "I can still see Mr. Bedwin, the laboratory superintendent, puffing through a long-stemmed clay pipe. His breath would go through condensing until he finally got fresh water."

In the *Beinn Bhreagh Recorder,* July 31, 1908, Bell noted: "One of our men at Beinn Bhreagh had two uncles whose dead bodies were picked up at sea in a dory. There was fish in the boat, but no water.

"It is certainly a reflection upon the intelligence of man that anyone should die of thirst upon the ocean; or that there should be 'Water, everywhere, nor any drop to drink.'

"Wherever there is water, there is water to drink; and it is only our ignorance that prevents us from taking a draught. Certainly, where fog exists there is plenty of fresh water at hand, in the air; and no one need die of thirst under such circumstances.

"Just consider what a fog means. It is fresh drinking water suspended in the atmosphere, half condensed, in the form of a visible cloud. All the fisherman has to do is to pump the fog into a bottle half submerged in the cold water of the ocean, and the fog will turn into fresh drinking water. . . .

"I tried the experiment of condensing drinking water from my breath . . . It is well known that water-vapour is one of the products of combustion of the lungs. If you breathe upon a mirror, or cold surface, water is immediately condensed upon the surface in the form of a mist, or fine dew.

"In this experiment I took an ordinary glass tumbler and holding it partly immersed in a bucket of cold water to keep it cool, I breathed into the tumbler.

"The open mouth of the tumbler almost completely covered my mouth; and I breathed in through the nose and out through the mouth.

"I kept this up for an hour or so, and as a result a considerable quantity of fresh water appeared at the bottom of the tumbler, showing the ease with which drinking water may be made with the simplest sort of apparatus if we can only get water vapor into a cool receiver."

"Speech—hearing—touch. He had so many things. You wonder how he had the brains to sort them out," Mayme Morrison Brown observes. "I don't think there's very much of anything he didn't try and a lot of it is used today. Birth control? He did say when talking about the overpopulated countries he wondered why scientists didn't come up with something.* And he was experimenting with heat and electricity. In Washington he had a great big place at the back of his house, and he had it piped around like a fridge for air cooling in the summer when the hot weather came. The iceman used to put hundreds of chunks of ice there. Great big pipes! Tons of ice! They put a table and chair down there for him—rugs and everything. It was lovely! You could go in there on the hottest day and find cool air. The iceman made money on it."

Bell foresaw the spiraling demand for energy; there were already shortages in his lifetime. (Mayme remembers him speaking of petroleum. "He used to say it could go as quickly as it came," she recalls.) Early in his career Bell began to identify directions in which our technological society would turn to seek relief. In 1878, with the telephone just on the market he wrote, "Can see clearly that study of laws of motion as applied to *Atoms* will lead to most valuable results taken in connection with Conservation of Energy. Strike clear of all pre-conceived ideas." Later his thoughts turned to solar heat. In the *Beinn Bhreagh Recorder* for January 17, 1914, he wrote, "The roofs of our houses afford wide expanses exposed to the sun, even in the most crowded cities. *Store* the heat by causing it to heat a liquid and lead the heated liquid into an insulated tank where it can be utilized at any time. . . . Tank on roof yields pressure that will carry fluid to any part of the house desired."

Bell thought about alternative energy to the end of his life. Melville Grosvenor recalled sitting on the couch beside his grandfather in the last autumn of his life at Beinn Bhreagh as he dictated a reply to a request to join in a New Year's symposium. The

* Conversations in Baddeck suggest that Bell may have conducted birth-control experiments but stopped them when his family objected.

question to be studied: What in 1922 will be the fields of study most in need of attention from American inventors and scientists? Bell's telegram of October 25, 1921, offered a suggestion:

"The cheap production of alcohol for power purposes, and the adaptation of machinery to be run by alcohol, instead of gasoline or steam, seems to me to be the subjects most worthy of study in 1922.

"The world's consumption of petroleum has become so enormous as to show that our supply cannot possibly last for many generations more. Coal and oil are strictly limited in quantity and can never be replaced when once removed from the earth. Wood, too, is difficult of reproduction as it takes 25 years to grow a crop of trees.

Helen Keller (far left) kneels beside Anne Sullivan Macy at a Bell family "harvest home" on the Beinn Bhreagh meadow, August 27, 1901.

79

Daisy with her apparatus for
maintaining artificial respiration, a
forerunner of the iron lung.
(Arthur McCurdy, 1898)

"The great hope of the future seems to lie in alcohol, a beautifully clean and efficient fuel which can be produced from sawdust, waste products of our farms and mills, from cornstalks and, in fact, from almost any vegetable capable of fermentation. Our growing crops and even weeds can be used. The waste products of our farms are all available and even the garbage from our cities.

"Other fuels, too, will eventually give out, but there is no reason why alcohol should not be cheaply produced and provide us with an inexhaustible source of power because it can be produced annually in any quantity desired."

"In the case of the lambs, both male and female, the size and position of the nipples with reference to each other was carefully noted and measured," wrote Mabel Bell of the sheep-breeding experiments. In the background is Sir Wilfred Grenfell.

Above:
Some of Bell's multi-nippled sheep, product of his longest-continued Beinn Bhreagh experiment. Bell kept a box of oats near the pasture gate and often fed them by hand.

Right:
Will Bedwin demonstrates a method for reclaiming water from exhaled breath, which Bell thought "as easy as smoking a pipe . . ."
(John Michael McNeil, 1909)

Attempting to revive a drowned sheep with the breathing apparatus. (Arthur McCurdy, 1898)

1907. Aug 12.

The Tetrahedron

"The thing he was interested in was how to make a stronger airplane wing. He was probably taken with Langley and all the others and he was trying to understand how he might do something better," another generalist, Buckminster Fuller, told me. "And he comes to discovering omni-triangulation. I call it the octahedron-tetrahedron truss. Then of course he went right on with his kites. . . . I knew absolutely nothing about it until I had discovered the same thing myself." The story of Bell's pioneering experiments on flight is also the story of the first discovery of the space frame.

Bell's interest in flight was lifelong. Thomas Watson, the "Mr. Watson, come here, I want you" of telephone fame, remembered that even while they worked on the telephone, Bell was eager to move on to the flying machine. In 1877, while on his honeymoon in England, he watched as "two or three hundred crows performed their evolutions only a few feet above my head," noticed particularly the action of their tails, scribbled some notes headed "Aerial navigation, Principles so far developed," and sketched a primitive diagram of a "flying machine." Perhaps ten years before the Wrights, Bell began actively working on flight; in his memoirs Charlie McCurdy remembered the early experiments in the barn on Crescent Grove.

At the time, after centuries of unproductive effort and frequent disaster, the ancient dream had fallen into disrepute, a subject for ridicule. Yet, as always, there were investigators. Notably, there was in the early nineties the gliding pioneer Otto Lilienthal of Germany, who, like would-be aviators from the very beginning of time, based his studies on the flight of birds and wrote *Birdflight as the Basis of the Flying Art;* there was Laurence Hargrave of Australia, who developed in 1892 a box kite with superior lifting power and stability; and there was in the United States Samuel Pierpont Langley, secretary of the Smithsonian Institution, who put his prestige behind the quest for flight, publishing in 1891 *Experiments in Aerodynamics* as one of the Smithsonian Contributions to Knowledge, and asserting, "The mechanical suspension of heavy

Opposite page:
High on his tetrahedral perch, Bell watches his kites in comfort. (John Michael McNeil, 1907)
Above:
Samuel P. Langley's steam-powered, propeller-driven airplane model in flight above the Potomac at Quantico, Virginia. (Alexander Graham Bell, May 9, 1896)

The windbreak, the world's first space frame. When covered with canvas, it formed a shield for assembling kites in the field. (George McCurdy, November 8, 1902)

Hector P. McNeil, patent holder with Bell of a device to connect tetrahedral cells, with one of the large cells made for the tetrahedral windbreak. (George McCurdy, August 30, 1902)

bodies in the air, combined with very great speeds, is not only possible, but within reach of mechanical means we actually possess."

Bell and Langley were friends, supporting and encouraging each other in experiments many considered unprofitable. The sight of Langley's test models in flight in 1891 caused Bell to say "It will be all UP with us someday" and to intensify his own experiments. By 1893 he was writing Mabel, "I am so full of 'flying machine' that I haven't put pen to paper for anything else. . . ." He tried out a helicopter apparatus, toying with fly wheels with rockets at the rotor tips, and experimented with wings and propellers.

Langley made several visits to Beinn Bhreagh, and Charles Thompson, Bell's butler, recollected them in his notes:

"During these years of studying, Prof. Langley spent several summers with Mr. Bell in Cape Breton Island. He was with Mr. Bell on several cruises with the houseboat. Sometimes no one else but Mr. Bell and Prof. Langley would be aboard for several days. I have seen them sitting on deck under the awning for hours and hours neither of them uttering a sound, but both of them eagerly watching the seagulls soaring about the boat. I remember one day Prof. Langley said suddenly in a raised voice, 'Isn't that maddening?' 'What's maddening,' said Mr. Bell. 'The gulls,' said Prof. Langley. 'I was thinking they were very beautiful,' Mr. Bell replied. They both eyed each other for a moment and then laughed heartily." (Aeronautical designers still watch the birds. Paul MacCready developed his innovative *Gossamer Condor*, which in 1977 made the first successful *man-powered* flight, partially as a result of observations he made while pursuing the age-old practice.)

In 1896 Bell watched Langley's successful trials of a steam-powered propeller-driven airplane model over the Potomac and he immediately wrote Langley, "I shall count this day as one of the most memorable of my life."

Bitter days were ahead for Langley, though. Financed by the U.S. War Department he went on to build a full-scale plane that was never actually tested in flight. On December 8, 1903, it caught in the launching ways on takeoff and crashed in the water before a jeering press that lampooned him until he became a national figure of fun.

But in 1896 Langley's triumph was a spur to aviation; and, ironically, so was the death that same year of Otto Lilienthal, fatally wounded when his glider stalled and crashed. He had made hundreds of glides—"communicating to the world," wrote Bell, "the results of his experiments with practical directions how to manage the machine under circumstances of difficulty." Other inventors benefited, among them Octave Chanute of Chicago, who built a sophisticated glider incorporating some of Lilienthal's ideas and who later befriended the Wright brothers. And in their bicycle shop in Dayton, Ohio, the mechanically adept Orville and Wilbur Wright, who were also admirers of Lilienthal, read about his death. The Wrights decided to study aviation, and in the course of their research visited public libraries and eventually wrote to the Smithsonian Institution for information.

In June 1899, the Wright brothers received in reply probably all the material on the subject on public record. They built a biplane kite, then a glider, then aviation's first wind tunnel—an open-ended wooden box, sixteen inches square on the inside by six feet long, in which they tested the air pressure on hundreds of miniature wings.

For his part, in 1896, the year of Langley's triumph and Lilienthal's death, Bell turned to kites, joining numerous experimenters before and since who have used the kite in pursuit of aerial flight (among the most recent: scientists with the National Aeronautics and Space Administration who developed kite-like devices for reentry of space vehicles). Bell was drawn to kites, which he called "lighter than air machines" (conversely, motor-propelled crafts were labeled "heavier than air"), because, as he wrote at Beinn Bhreagh on September 2, 1901, they permitted experiment without risk to human life. "The great difficulty in developing an art of aerial locomotion lies . . . in the difficulty of profiting by past experience. A dead man tells no tales. . . ."

Bell worked chiefly with kites based on the Hargrave box kite, the stability of which had made it immediately useful for meteorological purposes. In 1898 Bell had a Hargrave-type kite—15 feet long, nearly 11 feet wide, and 5 feet deep (suitably named Jumbo), and big enough to carry a man—built in his laboratory. However, Jumbo remained steadfastly earthbound. Eventually, the Nova Scotia–born astronomer Simon Newcomb, a friend of Bell's though he held negative views on the possibility of aerial flight, told him why in an article "Is the Air-ship Coming?" published in *McClure's Magazine* in September 1901:

"Let us make two flying machines exactly alike, only make one on double the scale of the other in all its dimensions. We all know that the volume, and therefore the weight, of two similar bodies are proportional to the cubes of their dimensions. The cube of two is eight: hence the large machine will have eight times the weight of the other. But surfaces are as the squares of the dimensions. The square of two is four. The heavier machine will therefore expose only four times the wing surface to the air, and so will have a distinct disadvantage in the ratio of efficiency to weight."

During the month of September, with "Is the Air-ship Coming?" and its negative answer to the query just off the press, Newcomb turned up at Beinn Bhreagh, rather startling his hosts, since Professor Langley (who was certain to disagree with Newcomb) was also a guest. But Newcomb had an attentive audience.

Bell picked some faults with Newcomb's principal argument—roughly, that an aircraft built twice as big would be eight times as heavy—but he wrote Mabel later that "Newcomb's law" had come as a "shock," casting doubt on the possibility of constructing flying machines unless "a new principle of support––momentum—was introduced." Still, he was not long despondent.

By the end of the month, in his fifty-fifth year, Bell had circumvented "Newcomb's law" and was on his way to a solution. He had embarked on a train of thought that would lead him to discovery of the tetrahedral cell.

It began with the idea that for greater lifting power he should fly *more* kites instead of *bigger* kites, the kites in question being his favored triangular box-types with cells of triangular section. The

One of Bell's experimental kites, with the Beinn Bhreagh laboratory in the background.

next step was to *compound* the kites, removing the extra stick where support sticks came together so that the compounded kites had the same lifting power as the individual kites but actually less weight.

In his notes for September 30, 1901, Bell reasoned: "By multiplying the number of our kites we can increase the lifting power indefinitely without weakening our construction and without altering the relation of surface to weight. Three kites for example would weigh just three times one kite and as they would have three times the surface, they would have three times the supporting power and they would be able together to support three times the additional load that could be carried by one. . . .

Bell and an assistant steady a kite.

"I see no doubt however that the kites would fly equally well if they were tied together at the corners. . . .

"*Ergo:* Do not increase the size of the cell, but compound small cells into a large structure, and where the two sticks come together omit one, and in this way the larger kites will have less weight relatively to their surfaces than the smaller kites, and yet be equally strong."

Within a few days Bell had assembled three triangular kites into a compound kite of hexagonal cross-section. The kite tested well, and he became confident that the next summer he could build a kite capable of lifting a man.

He was almost there; he needed only to push the idea a fraction further—the push would be a stroke of genius—to conceive the fundamental engineering structure basic today to building know-how all over the world. At that moment, however, the cells of Bell's compound kite were triangular prisms with two triangular and three rectangular faces. The rectangular faces still needed cross-bracing, adding, of course, additional weight to the structure. Back in Washington, D.C., that autumn and winter, Bell worked to find the lightest and most efficient method.

He had a number of models made up in a Washington workshop and finally put in an order for a hundred small rectangular panels with two sets of cross-bracing that he thought would enable him to make up prefabricated triangular kites right in the field. This was desirable, since he planned to continue work in the Washington area and transporting kites brought out the press; reporters had become a problem.

But before the panels were delivered, the idea of the tetrahedral cell and with it the device to connect cells together at the vertexes—today's universal connector—had struck him: "Avoid rectangular elements—let everything be built up of equilateral triangles," he wrote on March 15, 1902. "Terminal surfaces will then be at the proper angle to make connection with other frames. Whole thing could be built up into a solid compact form of almost any desired shape. . . ."

Bell sketched ideas for corner caps with holes for screw-in rods in his notebook. "We are all familiar with laboratory models of crystals composed of sticks or wires driven into peas," he noted. "Something like this is wanted—metallic wires and metallic (?) peas. . . ."

In these notes is the first description of the space frame. Perhaps the possibilities inherent in the idea did not occur to Bell at the time. But back in Beinn Bhreagh the following August the potential was clear in his mind. "Structures of this sort may be used in place of arches for bridges—ceilings of large buildings, etc. It lends itself to metallic structures. All the parts can be made of metal—and made cheaply."

Late summer and fall 1902 was one of the periods of greatest creativity for the Beinn Bhreagh laboratory. Workers began to construct tetrahedral skeletons, to cover the cells, and to turn out the connecting devices Bell had sketched in his notebooks. Hector P. McNeil, a Baddeck man who people remember "could make anything," was later to hold a joint patent with Bell for the connector.

Arthur McCurdy's oldest son, George, stood by to photograph each day's production. Bell glued into his album picture after picture, recording with meticulously dated snapshots each phase of development, writing neat notes into the margins.

The construction of large tetrahedral kites—true space frames—began. But, interestingly, Bell's first major tetrahedral construction was not a kite but a ground structure: a large windbreak for sheltering his kites. In photographs it sits on the Beinn Bhreagh meadow, a piece of premature High Tech sculpture. Mabel described it well in a letter to her mother: "The framework of the wind break is the same construction as he will employ for his next great kite and is so strong although so light and fragile looking that it will support him without sagging in the least and three men can lift it and him easily. Each piece of wood is only an inch thick and there are very few of them."

The frame took four men only one day to put in place. They covered it with a large sheet of canvas so that the big kites could be assembled in its shelter. The canvas, hinged to a roller, could be drawn back so that the wind would blow through to the kites.

Each day brought its problems—and often its solutions as well. Bell recorded in his notes for November 18, 1902: "Two great successes today, both a result of suggestions from Mabel.

"First suggestion. Instead of waiting for wind, attach kite to galloping horse. Tried it yesterday with small kites. So promising that we tried three of our large kites today in same way. Found I could study their mode of flight in the air as well as if I had wind—or nearly so—and could judge of their way of falling better than with wind."

Mabel's second suggestion involved using hairpins and sealing wax for building and linking tetrahedral skeletons; Bell pronounced this "just the thing." His enthusiasm for suggestion number one may have dwindled, however, since he noted a few days later that one of his large kites came to grief when "horse dragged it on road and broke some of the upper sticks."

Particularly sprightly photographs were taken the following autumn, in October 1903, when Bell switched from black spruce

This large tetrahedral kite was one of three that Bell raised aloft with the aid of a horse. (George McCurdy, November 19, 1902)

in his kites to strong but light aluminum tubing. Large kite frames were tossed up and about and supported effortlessly in the air; George McCurdy was there every time to snap the shutter. Bell maintained his laboratory photographic record with the same diligence that he took notes. He always had a laboratory member assigned to the job of "snapshotting" and had a permanent large photographic wooden backdrop erected near the laboratory. His interest may have been in scientific record but he also loved the drama of his tetrahedral kites, and in the heyday of kite flying he queried Mabel on her reaction to the idea of a book composed *solely* of photographs of kites. In addition to three McCurdys— Arthur and his sons D.G. (George) and D. or J.A.D. (Douglas)— laboratory employees whose names appear on photographs taken over the years include John Michael McNeil, Sam MacDonald, and E. H. Cunningham.

Bell developed many tetrahedral kite types. A favorite was the *Oionos,* named after the soaring birds from which the ancient Greeks drew their auguries. Bell began work with this kite form— which combined oblique and horizontal surfaces—in 1903 and

The kite and horse in motion. (George McCurdy, November 19, 1902)

Opposite page:
Testing the virtues of aluminum kite frames. (George McCurdy, October 16, 1903)

continued for years, since the kite demonstrated stability and lifting power. A dramatic but unsuccessful experiment was the ring kite, a flying circle that had a tendency to sideslip and crash. As work progressed the kites became huge in size.

Bell settled on standard ten-inch cells for his kites and nested them in great banks. They proved to give excellent stability in the air but they also created drag. Bell was not disturbed. He believed that the tetrahedral cell was the "brick" from which the safe, strong flying machine of the future would be built.

By 1905, when Mayme Morrison went to work in Bell's laboratory, the Wrights had flown (although in secret) and the race was on to build a viable aircraft. Mayme has lively memories of those exciting days and remembers just how the cells were made.

"There were quite a number in the laboratory by 1905. Most were there for the money. The only things going on then in Cape Breton were the fishing and coal mines, and the farmers just got by. There was nothing here unless someone started something, so it was a help to everyone. People had something to do; otherwise they weren't doing anything. They weren't paid too much money, but then you could live so much easier—cheaper. You had your own eggs and your own vegetables, and you grew your own meat.

"There were thirty or forty employed in the lab and the annex. The boat, the *Gauldry,* used to bring people over from Baddeck. A lot of people remember the *Gauldry;* fifteen or sixteen or maybe more used to come over. If they didn't meet the boat, they'd dock them for being late. They couldn't dock me. . . . I lived over at Red Head anyway!

"There were a lot of girls from Baddeck: Mary MacIvor—the little widow MacIvor we used to call her—Minnie Morrison, Tina

take 1903C #10

319 DSM 1903C #11

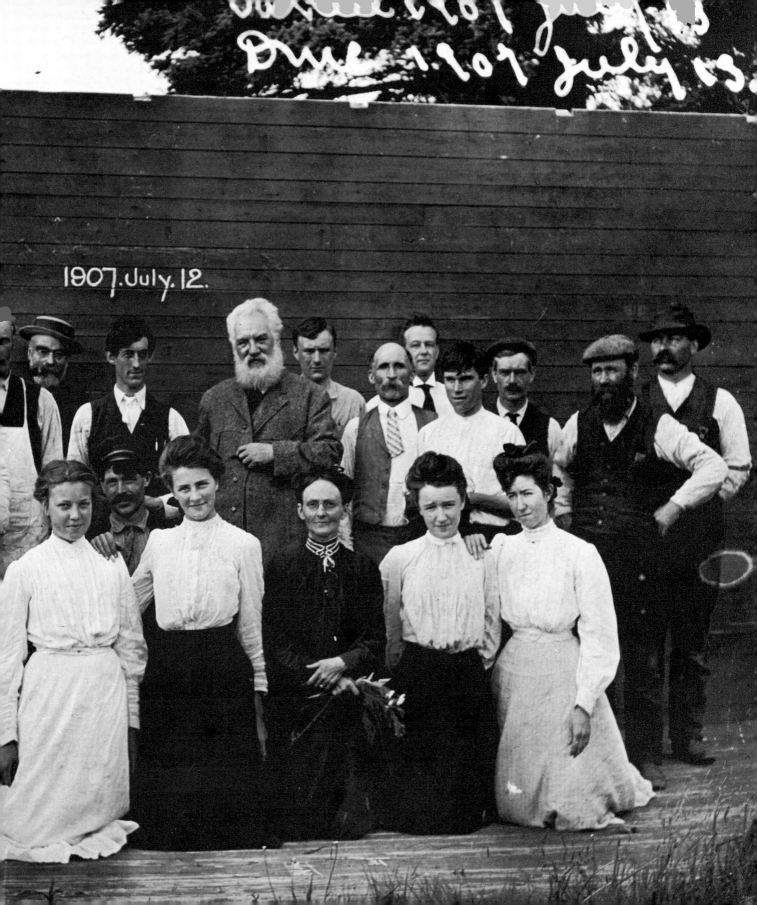

1907. July. 12.

MacLean Connick, Annie Watson MacInnes, Annie Mae Murphy from Baddeck; Katie MacDermid and Cassie MacDermid of Baddeck Bay; a Fleming girl—Annie Fleming from Margaree.

"Dr. Bell was testing then to get something heavier than air—experimenting with the tetrahedron.

"The laboratory was up on a bank with everything run by water power, and there was an annex where we made the kites and cells and other things. They did an awful lot of carpentry there. They cut all their own wood. I remember they had saws going in the back room.

"There was a superintendent—first it was Angus Ferguson and then Will Bedwin from North Sydney. He just showed you something for a minute and that was it. You'd get the cells—the little wooden structures—and you'd sew the silk on those. That's what made the cells. They were not exactly triangles . . . they had three faces that were covered and one underneath all open.

"Dr. Bell used to walk down from the Point House to the laboratory every day at noon. He'd work at night in his study at the Point House and sometimes he'd go to bed when others would get up. But you'd see him strolling down to the laboratory around lunchtime—every blessed day. That was his walk. At first he had his office at the side of the annex where all the people were working.

"Some people thought him cranky. Well, anyone would be once in a while but it was unusual. I never saw him lose his temper. He could be sarcastic; if something didn't strike him right he could give a sarcastic answer. He could cut you off at the pockets. Oh, he could! Many's the time he'd check Mr. Bedwin, the laboratory superintendent, because Mr. Bedwin kind of ran things his own way.

"We used to pile up hundreds of cells. They were all made from red silk. Dr. Bell imported the silk—hundreds of webs.

"They were easy to do. You'd use more or less a buttonhole stitch—somewhat tighter. You'd fold the silk right in and buttonhole it along the wood so the wind wouldn't tear it. You'd put the stitches probably an eighth of an inch apart. You'd just run along and do them in jig time. By hand. There were no machines. A machine wouldn't do that properly.

"In those days they had their own sheep and their own wool and their own looms and they hooked all their own rugs. They did all their own quilting and sometimes they did some for exhibitions. The day they'd be taking the quilt out of the frame—that was a real party! But so long as you knew how to buttonhole, you didn't need to sew. Except for one girl who was a dressmaker, no one was a special seamstress.

"One time I was put on the cutting table because the girl we had doing it was wasting a lot of material. I don't know why he stuck me on there because I could waste too. But I cut for part of the summer. I saw it wasn't wasted. We were afraid someone might walk off with some of it, too. It was really beautiful material—great big webs. I don't know how many yards. Red and white. We didn't use too much white. But one of the kites—I think it was the *Cygnet*—had part white, just a few cells at either end. But they didn't photo well, so he favored red in all the kites he made.

"What I liked doing was putting the cells together. I worked at a little bench. We'd sit there and gab and do it very quickly. They were made out of spruce or any kind of good wood. You'd pinch a little metal on them at the top and at the corners with a little hand machine.

"One time I was putting the cells together with Hector P. McNeil and old Michael MacLean, and Sam Watson made some little lever you'd put your foot on and it would do it for you. That was his invention to make it easier for us. He and I were working together . . . getting far ahead of the others, using his machine. It was great fun.

"Just last week, one morning, someone came up here to see me and said, 'Can you identify this?' There was nothing to it. It was the little hand machine we used for snapping the metal on the cells. They'd found it in Hector P.'s old barn.

"There was a competition between us girls. I asked Mr. Bedwin, 'Is it all right?' and he said, 'Yes, it is.' Whoever did the most cells in the week—you had your own place to pack—would get a long weekend or a day off. There was a Murphy girl there—Annie Mae Murphy—who was a little older than I and the others. She cheated all the time. I went in one morning and looked back where the cutting table was and said, 'That pile of mine has gone down. It was way up over the table.' Mrs. MacIvor wasn't satisfied and some had been taken from Tina Connick. We couldn't find who did it. We looked around, and Annie Mae Murphy was hiding way in the back. She had taken them to get a day off! But we got her! When Tina was going home and we were down at the wharf just before Tina got on the boat, we dumped Annie Mae over the wharf!

"We left her there and said, 'That's what you get for stealing our cells. Tomorrow is supposed to be your day off!'

"Oh, there was a nice staff of girls. Lively, most of them. Dr. Bell loved everybody to be happy. Just loved it. I remember the day we had the picture taken of all the girls in the laboratory. That was 1907, I think. Dr. Bell stood behind me. I'm so tall I had

John Michael McNeil, one of the assistants who photographed trials of Bell's experimental air and water craft in a picture taken about 1908.

Sam MacDonald, who worked in the laboratory and photographed for Bell. (About 1910)

to kneel. I said, 'Is this the first time, Dr. Bell, you've had a girl down on her knees before you?' He laughed so hard!

"I got a dollar a day. That was good money. The others were paid fifty cents a day, and I don't know why but Mr. Bedwin said, 'We're going to pay you a dollar a day but don't you tell the others.' Well, I certainly wasn't going to tell. Mrs. Bell wrote the checks, and she didn't say anything. It was just because I used to run up to the kite house when Dr. Bell was there and I'd sit and talk to him and take notes from him or some little thing for probably an hour.

"He was good with young people; he had a nice way of telling you what you had to do."

Getting into the Air

Bell's conception of a kite capable of lifting a man was not an impossible one. In China, where kites almost certainly originated, stories dating from earliest times attest that both man-lifting and man-carrying kites—enthusiasts note an important distinction—were flown, frequently for military purposes. In the nineteenth century, prior to Bell's efforts, at least two Englishmen had built man-lifting kites. But Bell's man-lifter, his *Frost King*, tested in December 1905, was to have an important advantage. As he often explained, "Here is the point of the tetrahedral structures . . . they have automatic stability." In fact, in time he expected to construct what, because of the aerodynamics, had been left untried in the West: a man-carrier, with ample room in its tetrahedral corpus to accommodate passengers—and engine.

Mayme Morrison Brown was often there when the kites were being tested. "They assembled the kites in the annex as we finished or in the hangar. Then the men would carry them up to the kite field. All that area above the lodge was clear then—there were no spruce and no trees there. It's all grown up now, but it was all bare ground up there. The observation house was just a little tentlike shape, and they used to watch from there. They'd have one or two anchor posts—just a post with pulleys for ropes on it. They'd have the men that were working there on the ropes, and according to how the wind was they'd let the rope out—yards and yards of rope that went through on the pulleys stuck in the field. They'd test one kite at a time, and there'd be three or four men. If I remember right, they had three guide lines. Dr. Bell would keep check on the air and the weight of the machine. He didn't say much, but in his own scrawly way he marked down about it—if you could read his writing. He made an awful lot of scribbling on a lot of things.

"The men would wait for the squalls of wind to die down, and then they'd take them in and land them right on the field. When there was no wind, they'd come down very easily. But each man on the rope had to be careful. One wouldn't pull harder than the other.

An *Oionos* kite held ready for launching. Bell began experimenting with this favorite type, named for the great soaring birds from which the Greeks drew their auguries, in 1903. The combination of oblique and horizontal surfaces provided stability and lifting power. Red silk ties along the cord enhanced its visibility. (William Nutting, 1904)

Mabel Bell measuring kite pull by means of a scale attached to the kite cord. (George McCurdy, 1903)

"Well, it was beautiful, you know . . . testing the lighter-than-air machines. There were so many kites, so many that never had names. They were experiments. They were really beautiful in the clear sky . . . usually in the late afternoon when the sun was going down. He loved to see them fly. 'Beautiful,' he'd say. 'Beautiful.'

"The *Frost King* . . . that was a beautiful kite. One of the largest. I don't know how many hundred cells there were in it . . . an awful lot. That's the one that picked the man up—Neil MacDermid, Kenny MacDermid's uncle. That was a surprise; it really was. It picked him up unbeknownst to him.

"Well, I think Dr. Bell knew it was going that day. They let the guy ropes go! The day it happened we were up in the little observation house. Dr. Bell's father was there lying on a cot—old Melville Bell was a fine old man; he had big whiskers just like Dr. Bell but he didn't have Dr. Bell's keen black eyes—and Melville Grosvenor, he was always with his grandfather when he was a tot of three or four. And I think Dr. Bell and I were standing there, too. I had the camera, anyway. I remember I snapped them in the observation house.

"I took about everything that stood or moved with that old Brownie. Everyone was taking pictures then. If you had a friend anywhere, you'd have two or three pictures of them. We took pictures of most everything that was going on around there. Usually everyone got a copy.

"That day there were heavy squalls. A gust of wind comes—maybe from the west—a guy rope slips, and away she goes! Neil went up at least thirty feet hanging from the rope. Oh, they said it was more because he was scared to death. It was the end of the world for him.

"Dr. Bell was quite excited that it had picked him up. Oh, it was perfectly safe. Dr. Bell knew he wasn't going to get hurt—there was nothing to hurt him. But Neil was petrified. You'd think it was a terrible disaster. I can hear Dr. Bell yet. He threw up his hands . . . he enjoyed it.

"Neil dangled there for quite a little while before they took him down. He thought he was up a thousand feet! We used to tease him about it.

"I snapped pictures. I took a picture of the man in the air . . . a picture of Neil on the rope. John Michael McNeil and I developed the pictures in a little darkroom there in the annex. There was nothing to it. You'd just put them in the proper solution and use the proper light.

"But Neil didn't like anybody seeing that picture. They made up stories about him . . . that he'd peed in his pants! He was furious.

Bell takes notes as assistants man the anchor post. (Sam MacDonald, 1908)

"Oh, there were all kinds of pictures. But nobody seemed to think they would be history today."

Two other versions of Neil MacDermid's feat exist. Neil's own comments, with overtones that are just a little grumpy, were recorded for posterity by Ron MacInnis in 1974 for the Canadian Broadcasting Corporation. "I was working down in the garden and they sent for me and I went up and they had everything rigged up . . . so they told me to ketch hold of the rope and I went . . . caught hold of the rope and Mr. Bell hollered out for to hold on to it, hold on to it . . . so the first thing I knew I was up in the air . . . then he commenced hollering for to pull me down, pull me down . . . he hollered for me not to let the rope go. So I got down on the ground and that was all there was to it. I went back to my work after that. Well, he gave me five dollars when I got down—that was all I got. . . ."

On December 28, 1905, Mabel Bell wrote one of her lively letters to Arthur McCurdy, Bell's former secretary, whose son Lucien had taken a previous glide on the *Frost King*. (Apparently Lucien was picked to be the first, although his flight was not photographed.) It was generally believed in Baddeck that Neil's ride was an accident, but Mabel Bell's letter makes it clear that, as Mayme Morrison Brown suspected, Bell knew the *Frost King* was "going" that day; he had postponed his return to Washington, D.C., and was waiting impatiently for favorable winds.

"I have started several letters to you," Mabel wrote, "but it seems as if I had had scarcely time for anything but sleeping, eating and doing things that had to be done.

"First, I must ask you and Hattie's congratulations on Mr. Bell's final triumph—Lucien's exploit when he hung suspended above ground simply sufficed to show what the *Frost King* could do, and was as much as could have been accomplished without previous preparation. It was perfectly satisfactory to Mr. Bell at the time and we would very likely have gone home before but that Mr. Cunningham, the photographer, had chosen just that time to lock himself in the darkroom and develop some rather worthless pictures of Susie and Jack, and there was no other camera available, so the event passed unrecorded pictorially.

"While a strong wind was not required—in fact I was not aware at the time that there was any—*more* wind was necessary, and day succeeded day and, although the lake was not always like glass, the few intermissions generally occurred at night or were too short to avail.

"Finally on Christmas day a breeze came playing hide and seek and got caught sufficiently long to allow His Majesty to ascend in all his stately dignity and hover serenely above the hilltop,

Kite watching. Alexander Graham Bell with his eldest grandchild, Melville Grosvenor. (Gilbert Grosvenor, 1908)

A tetrahedral ring kite was tested in 1907–1908, but the form was abandoned after it showed tendencies to sideslip and crash. (Gilbert Grosvenor, 1908)

but not long enough to admit of Lucien's ascending the rope ladder it had carried above when the men had pulled it down to be within his reach. You see, the kite went up itself about 300 metres [980 feet], carrying the rope ladder which commenced about 30 feet (10 metres) below and hung down 14 feet (5 metres); and in order to enable Lucien to reach the lowest rung it had to be pulled down, but before the men could get it down the wind gave out and the *King* came down of his own accord and ended all experiments for the day. Douglas got good photographs in spite of the biting cold, but of course there was no spectacular aeronaut to snap shot.

"The boys got discouraged and left next morning to our great regret, but we hung on desperately. More days of waiting followed; then Mr. Bell got more and more desperate and took to getting up early, and this morning just as we were finally giving up and going South he was rewarded. The wind was not a good one, in fact he says it was the worst possible, and Ferguson at the laboratory and Davidson at the Point said no use trying, but he went—a forlorn hope as again the lab was deserted except for Ferguson.

"There being no lightweight men I offered my 115 [pounds] and Mr. Bell would have accepted but, of course, there were any number of last things to do, with no one to help, so I remained. Just as the trunks descended the stairs Mr. Bell burst into the office (formerly Daisy's room) waving the Kodak. 'Develop, develop,' he cried. 'We've got him, and if the photos don't come out I'm not going today!' And he hustled me off downstairs to the darkroom.

"Of course I had ordered it tidied up that very morning and we lost precious time and nerve finding the developing powder but finally succeeded. Davidson mixed mine all right and I went ahead slowly and calmly in spite of Mr. Bell popping in and out the door, jumping about like a boy, and his three pictures came out beautifully, but only showed Neil MacDermid just clear of the ground. However, that was enough, and there was rejoicing and the trunks started and I went off to finish.

"Meanwhile, Davidson went on with his photographs which were to show Neil in all the splendor of his 30 feet of elevation. Alas and alas, in the excitement he got hold of the wrong developer (the slow one, I believe) and when I came back I found him almost literally tearing his hair and very certainly slapping his thigh and shaking himself in high disgust and indignation in having spoiled his beauties. If only . . . I had been there we might have helped him save something, for the developer is perfectly good only he did not know it, and in despair had put his film in the hypo.

"I wanted Mr. Bell to wait another day and try again as the wind still held . . . but he refused! Said those he had were sufficient. I have since found out he was too nervous to stand the strain again for he said, 'You've no idea how high up he was. You don't know how high 30 feet is, it's more than twice the height of the telegraph poles, and if the rope had broken or anything on the kite had given away and Neil had fallen he would have been killed or seriously injured.'

"Mr. Bell hadn't meant him to go quite so high apparently; anyway he was thankful the ascent and descent had been accomplished safely without hitch or trouble anywhere, and he'd no mind to risk fortune again.

"Now, as for the facts. The *Frost King* is a comparatively small and light kite. The figures as given in the newspaper account Mr. Bell sent you are fairly correct, and on this occasion it supported in the air, 30 feet from the ground, Neil weighing 165 lbs. and ropes and rope ladder bringing the total weight carried *outside* its own [to] 226 lbs. And this in a wind of no great strength, just a fair sailing breeze coming from the worst kite quarter so poor that

Neil MacDermid about to ride 30 feet in the air on the *Frost King*. "I made the first flight," he would tell friends in later years. His kite ascension occurred four years before the first aircraft flight in Canada. (Alexander Graham Bell, December 28, 1905)
Right:
Ring kite. (Gilbert Grosvenor, 1908)

Ferguson telephoned Mr. Bell that there was no use in coming down to try it. . . .

"Mr. Bell is so happy and so excited underneath a very quiet demeanor—it means so terribly much to him. . . . We've just lived for this moment. Day after day we've gone to the window and turned away in despair and everyone and everything has been waiting for it. We've just existed while waiting. Susie's wedding and the boys' visit just relieved the tension a bit, but it's been awful and I'm glad we are still alive and kicking."

Walter (Jack) Frost and his bride, Susan McCurdy, with the *Frost King,* December 16, 1905. The immense kite, with its 1,300 red silk cells, was named in celebration of their marriage.

With the trial of the man-lifter accomplished, Bell began working in the summer of 1906 on kites that could be launched and landed on the water, since he believed this approach would provide the greatest safety for testing the tetrahedral machine on which he now began to concentrate. But he found that he could not make watertight floats; when the kite rose from the water, it carried water within it. The solution was to send the kite up not from the water but from a boat under tow. This caused him to start experimenting with a life raft supported on two metal cylinders, each two feet in diameter and fifteen feet long, and propelled by aerial propellers.

Mayme Morrison sometimes participated in the trials. "While Dr. Bell was experimenting with the kites he was also experimenting on the water with the two copper floats we called the *Ugly Duckling* . . . two great copper pontoons with a platform with a motor and propeller to catch the wind. He found out something as far as speed was concerned with that machine. When it speeded, it raised just a little out of the water. I imagine he was thinking of takeoff for planes. There were four or five of us who would go out on it and speed the full length of the pond and go like sixty. A lot of the girls wouldn't even offer. The water would spray! I used to love to go out and get soaking wet and then come home and have coffee.

"When he tested with the kites on the water, it was somewhat different to testing in the field. Some of the kites he tested with the *Blue Hill* steamer drawing them for speed. They'd do it whenever they could get the steamer. He'd gauge just by looking at the different positions the kites would take on the wind as they were piloted from below. There were several they towed on the water."

One day as Mayme and I continued our interviews I learned that Catherine MacDermid, daughter of the *Blue Hill*'s Captain MacDonald, lived in a yellow frame house with big verandas down the street. Did she have memories of the *Blue Hill*? Indeed she did—many fond memories. "The *Blue Hill* was the dearest boat," she declared. "She was a lady among the lake boats." Sometimes after school the young Catherine would stand on deck when the big red kites under tow sailed overhead.

"Every day they made two trips to Iona from Baddeck to meet the trains with the mail and the passengers. I often went with my father—it was easy enough to go after school. During the hours when the boat was in Baddeck, Dr. Bell used to take the chance to use the *Blue Hill* to tow the experimental kites in the wind. There were all different designs and often they'd crash. My sister Ollie and I would gather up the cells and make dolls' clothes with the red silk."

A pontoon-equipped kite takes a ducking. (Douglas McCurdy, July 13, 1907)

By 1906 Bell was working on kites that could be launched and landed on water. The experiment was set back when he discovered he could not make watertight floats, so he began to launch them from rafts under tow.

Right:
Aboard the tow boat, Bell (right) watches a kite lift off from the *Ugly Duckling.* (Douglas McCurdy, August 9, 1907)

Positioning a kite on the *Ugly Duckling.* (Douglas McCurdy, August 9, 1907)

Flight

The successful flight of the *Frost King* with 165-pound Neil Mac-Dermid carried unwillingly along brought an end to most of Bell's experiments with kites. He felt he could now put a tetrahedral flying machine—the strongest and safest kind, he believed—in the air. In 1906 he and Mabel began seeking qualified young men to work with him to achieve this goal. At the same time, the Bells were keenly aware of the wider engineering potential in tetrahedral construction. Mabel had pushed her husband to patent his tetrahedral discovery, and on September 20, 1904, he received patent no. 770,626 for "aerial vehicle or other structure." He also was granted a joint patent with his assistant Hector P. McNeil for the tetrahedral connector. Bell had hoped to interest Charlie Bell, his Washington banker cousin, in the system's commercial development and was disappointed when he failed to do so. However, Mabel had obtained favorable opinions from engineering consultants and was determined that she and her husband would proceed on their own.

In the summer of 1906 the twenty-four-year-old Frederick W. (Casey) Baldwin, a college friend of Arthur McCurdy's second son, Douglas, and a new graduate of the University of Toronto, arrived at Beinn Bhreagh, never to leave again for very long.

In a letter to her mother on November 11, 1906, Mabel wrote "We are quite swell these days with the grandson of one of 'Canada's great statesmen' [Sir Robert Baldwin, a pre-Confederation premier of Upper Canada] working in our forge. . . .

"It is such a lovely thing for me to see my husband at last, before it is too late, working in company with a capable young man who so thoroughly believes in him and his latest invention that he is staking his whole future on it and bringing his friends in also.

"This young fellow, Mr. Baldwin, is building a lookout tower for Alec on top of the mountain. It would be a great piece of extravagance but Alec must have his system worked out practically in some way so as to learn by practical experience its weak points and remedy them, that we may go before the commercial world

117

ready to begin with the assurance of success. I hoped Charles would have been willing to form a small working company to share the expense with Alec as he did the Volta Graphophone Association but since he has not, Alec and I have gone on by ourselves and now this young man is coming in with his friends and he is as enthusiastic and confident as Alec and has inspired his friends with the like enthusiasm."

Mayme Morrison Brown remembers the young assistant. "Mr. Baldwin came down here as a student. He was down in the laboratory doing what he could there. Dr. Bell said he would keep him on if he would build a tetrahedral tower. He challenged him . . . he was testing him to see if he was really interested . . . to see what he could do as an engineer. So I think it was 1907 that the tower was finished. Baldwin built it—tetrahedral on a concrete base. It was all put together like tetrahedral cells. Like the kite cells.

Casey Baldwin (center) directing erection of the tetrahedral tower. Two of the three legs were assembled on the ground to form a V and the structure was gradually jacked up as the third leg was constructed tier by tier. (Douglas McCurdy, 1907)

The iron work—strong iron bars—was done in Dr. Bell's own laboratory. It was ninety or a hundred feet. Dr. Bell was very proud of it.

"Why was it built? Just to prove that the structure would be strong and safe. And it was! That was Mr. Baldwin's success in the laboratory. The tower proved the tetrahedron was strong. The tetrahedral tower was up on the top of the mountain. There were steps but you had to have good courage to go up there. Goodness, the tourists!

"Dr. Bell's grave is there now."

By 1907 Bell had four enthusiasts for flight at his side: Douglas McCurdy; Casey Baldwin; Glenn Curtiss, twenty-nine, at the time a small-town pioneer manufacturer of motorcycles and motorcycle engines; and Lieutenant Thomas E. Selfridge, twenty-five, on loan from the U.S. Army. They were not as convinced as Bell about the use of the tetrahedral "brick" in the flying machine of the future but, wrote Mabel Bell to her mother, "They have brightened and youngened Alec wonderfully."

The Aerial Experiment Association (A.E.A.) was formed on October 1, 1907. The object of the association, Bell explained in a speech to the American Philosophical Society two years later, was "to get into the air! We had heard that the Wright Brothers had gotten into the air at Dayton, Ohio, and we believed it to be true." Bell's man-carrying tetrahedral kite-plane was to be the association's first project; after that, the four associates might develop independent designs. At the outset, as it has been noted, none had seen an airplane; by the time the association was dissolved in March 1909, its members could claim among their contributions to the infant science of aviation the tricycle undercarriage and independent development of the aileron. And, perhaps most impressively, they built in under eighteen months four of the world's first workable aircraft. Financing came from Mabel Bell: $35,000 of her own money.

Mayme told me of these beginnings: "They started trying to get an engine that was light enough to place in the kite. They were trying everything to get a heavier-than-air machine that would fly. Glenn Curtiss was interested, and Dr. Bell had him working, experimenting with engines, and he made different engines for different machines.

"The first time I ever saw a motorcycle, Glenn Curtiss had it. They were using some of his motors in the experiments, and Glenn was down for quite a while. I remember the first ride on the motorbike. I hopped on behind Glenn Curtiss. We were testing the time around the high-level road and back to the laboratory again. Eleven miles of road. We got back, and just as he turned we struck something and I went way up in the woods. We made good time anyway. Dr. Bell timed us."

Of the four young associates, Glenn Curtiss's career in aviation was to be the most spectacular. The lightweight engines designed in the motorcycle factory he established in 1902 helped the aeronautical industry to make great progress early in its existence. In 1909 Curtiss formed, with A. M. Herring, the first aircraft manufacturing company in the United States. He died in 1930, regarded as the greatest American aviation pioneer next to the Wright brothers—and a millionaire to boot.

The testing of the A.E.A.'s first craft—Bell's giant tetrahedral kite, the *Cygnet*—took place on December 6, 1907. The kite was tested under tow by the *Blue Hill* and had Tom Selfridge as passenger. "He was a lovely person," remembers Mayme. "Tall and nice-looking, kind of a dark skin. So interesting."

The flight, during which Selfridge lay prone in a central cell space, was intended as a practice glide before installation of an engine. But after several minutes of smooth sailing, smoke from the steamer's funnel hid the man-carrier's descent, so that the tow line remained uncut. This caused the big kite to be dragged on impact, scattering its 3,400 red silk cells on the water. Selfridge dived clear, and Bell declared himself satisfied with the kite's performance in the air. Although not all shared his belief in a plane of tetrahedral design, he decided to order manufacture of more cells to ready a *Cygnet II* for powered trials the next summer.

Selfridge had escaped unharmed, but the accident proved to be a precursor of tragedy. Nine months later, on September 17, 1908, Selfridge crashed while flying as a passenger with Orville Wright at Fort Myer, Virginia, and became modern aviation's first fatality. Mabel Bell had held him in special affection. After his death she wrote to her mother, "I don't think any of you ever realized how near and dear Tom and the other boys were to me. For the others, including Alec, my relation was more or less of caring for them. *He* cared for me, looked after me in a hundred little ways I have never been looked after before. I know he loved me very much, not more and perhaps not as much as the others, but he was a different kind of man, the man who takes care of women and children."

After the trial of the *Cygnet*, the A.E.A. moved operations to Hammondsport, New York, where Glenn Curtiss had his motorcycle factory. There Curtiss, Selfridge, Baldwin, and McCurdy started gliding practice as preparation for designing their first aircraft. Bell visited and kept in touch. In his definitive biography *Bell*, Robert V. Bruce says, "He contributed significantly to the step-by-step improvement of successive aircraft and especially to

Bell, Mabel, grandson Melville, and Baldwin at ceremonies honoring the opening of the tower. (Caroline McCurdy, August 31, 1907)

Wheels. Charles Thompson, Bell's butler, chauffeurs Douglas McCurdy (front seat), Casey Baldwin, and Bell. (About 1908)

the analysis and remedy of failures." Pileups were routine, but in quick succession the A.E.A. built its pioneering aircraft: the *Red Wing*, the *White Wing*, the *June Bug*, and the *Silver Dart*. Construction was under the supervision first of William P. Bedwin, superintendent of Bell's Beinn Bhreagh laboratory, and later of Kenneth Ingraham, another member of the laboratory staff. Casey Baldwin was the first to pilot both the *Red Wing* and the *White Wing*. His initial flight in the *Red Wing* was credited by aviation pioneer Octave Chanute as the first public flight in America of a "heavier-than-air machine." (Unlike the Wrights, who avoided publicity, the A.E.A. members were not averse to an audience.)

The fourth A.E.A. plane was the *Silver Dart*. It incorporated all that the A.E.A. had learned. Canadian historian Richard Lindo, who directed the interpretation of the Bell exhibits in the Alexander Graham Bell National Historic Park, describes the *Silver Dart* as the most sophisticated aircraft in the world at the time of its construction. "Historians of aviation tend to overlook the important contributions of the A.E.A.," he notes, "because the Wrights had done so much to develop the art before Bell and his associates began. The fact is that Bell and his colleagues, independent of the Wrights, made important discoveries relating to the control and motive power of aircrafts. Their discoveries were embodied in the *Silver Dart*."

After initial testing, the *Silver Dart* was shipped to Baddeck. (When it ran into customs difficulties, the citizenry sent a wire to authorities in Ottawa: FREE ENTRY ON EXPERIMENTAL FLYING MACHINE.) Then on February 23, 1909, over the Bras d'Or ice, the *Silver Dart* made the first Canadian plane flight with Baddeck's native son Douglas McCurdy as pilot.

After a career in aviation, McCurdy, more formally known as J. A. D. McCurdy, would become lieutenant governor of Nova Scotia. Mayme recalls his readiness for adventure:

"People will still tell you stories about Douglas McCurdy. It still goes strong. He used to get very drunk, you know. Douglas was the first to have a car down here. Built high like the old Fords used to be. I called it the High Priest. He had that old car for so long . . . he liked it. He was coming from the Baldwins at Red Head one night and ran it right off the bridge down into the brook and he was there all night. Next time I saw him he had his salt-and-pepper suit on and I said, 'Are you going to the bridge tonight, Douglas?' Poor Dougie. He was born here, he lived here, his people were here. Douglas and his brother George and I palled around together when we were kids. They used to be regular little devilkins . . . always around in their boat.

"The day of his flight was a cold day in February. Cold! It was cold as charity.* We were near froze on the ice. But people came from everywhere. Some were on skates . . . the ice was covered. Dr. and Mrs. Bell were there with their horse and riding sleigh with fur robes around them. I stood on the back of the runners. The men pulled the *Silver Dart* out with a sleigh. Dr. Bell wouldn't show any excitement. He was registering everything with those black eyes of his, but he wouldn't show anything. Mrs. Bell was the one to get excited; she'd clap her hands! Dr. Bell said, 'Douglas is going to fly.' Douglas McCurdy was wearing just a little suit coat over his shirt; he wasn't equipped. He went up in that

---

* Some who attended brought with them another new invention: the Thermos.

little suit coat to test the *Silver Dart.* I said to Dr. Bell, 'He's the only fool on the ice who'd go up in that little suit coat!' Well, he flew quite a bit. He made a name for himself. Nerve! Douglas would try anything.

"Dr. Bell thought the flight was wonderful. He was pleased. He remarked that it would have gone further but for a squall of wind that took it down.

"There's one thing he did say—over and over again: he never wanted his work to be used for war. He always hoped his work would be used to benefit people.

"But the first thing we knew was the First World War with sea planes here in Cape Breton and the air force."

Members of the Aerial Experiment Association: Glenn H. Curtiss, Casey Baldwin, Bell, Lieutenant Thomas E. Selfridge, J. A. D. McCurdy. (Mabel Hubbard Bell, 1907)

Norman Bethune, who some years later opened Baddeck's first gas station, was a witness to the first flight. "Bessie MacDonald, our teacher, said there'd be people coming from Ottawa and all over and she didn't see why Baddeck people couldn't see too," he remembers. "She let the class out, so a few of us went down. We carried our skates to the shore and went across the ice. So I was there at the first flight.

"My father was there with my young brother Tabbie in the sleigh. McCurdy, who I knew very well, went over to speak to them. But I was on skates, skating around to look at what they were doing—and to see if I could smell the gasoline. You know, the gasoline had a pleasant odor about it—more like benzine—very pleasant."

Dan Stewart, whose father William was Beinn Bhreagh's chief carpenter—his black beard distinguishes him in many kite photographs—used to hear his father's descriptions of the day's events. "My father worked in the lab where all the experimental work was carried on. He was a pretty good skater and he was one of those who followed the *Silver Dart* on the ice, on a pair of homemade stock skates—blacksmith's files ground and sharpened and inserted into wood with slots for straps to fasten on the toes and around the back. That's what a lot of them had at the time. . . . At a given signal the engines started up and when the *Dart* started to fly the workmen who were around it all skated behind it for quite a distance."

Dan Stewart missed the first flight himself but he saw the second. "The following day McCurdy and the *Dart* made a long flight. They went up the lake and they went a mile or so along the shore and we watched it all through the schoolhouse window. They weren't flying high, but it was wonderful to see. Yes, it was a novelty—something to wonder about."

In his notes, Bell wrote for February 23, 1909:

> Red letter day
> McCurdy flew over Baddeck
> Bay in the *Silver Dart*
> about one half mile

The writing was larger than usual and more flamboyant, but the day was not without irony and disappointment for Bell, as Mabel knew well.

On the day preceding the flight of the *Silver Dart*, Bell had tested his giant tetrahedral plane, the *Cygnet II*. Norman Bethune remembers watching the trial. "I was over there every day and I saw them try with the kite—two or three runs. They didn't get it up. It was quite large; at least as large as this room and all red.

125

They pushed it out from the shed; there was a space for the person to sit in and the motor I think was behind."

The big kite-plane stayed on the ground. Mabel Bell had feared this result. In fact, two days before its trial she had predicted it. In a letter to her mother she wrote: "I am counting the days till I can see you and at the same time dreading to leave Alec. He is well and bright but it is a great disappointment that the new engine is too heavy and not powerful enough to do much for his aerodrome.

"It looks very much like a case of the old *Great Eastern,* all right in itself but with not the proper motive power. However, Alec is not discouraged. I don't believe he ever will be. We are to try and see what the drome will do with this engine tomorrow.

"Probably nothing will happen and then there will be the old round of experimental drudgery to be gone over again. Of course there are lots of things that can be done. Alec himself has never been particularly sanguine about the practicality of the pure tetrahedral shape for it has less lifting power than any other, but it is so beautifully steady in the air. You can't conceive what a beautiful object these great big red silk kites are in the air. They are so solid and substantial and seem just glued to one place in the sky while all round the wind is whirling past making tall trees bend. I am sure it will come out all right in the end and there's no question but that this is the steadiest and strongest form."

But aircraft design took a different direction. Bell's red silk kites have been called a spectacular backdrop against which the infant aeronautical industry matured. None of Bell's great tetrahedral kite-planes—*Cygnet II* or the later *Oionos* and *Cygnet III* ever managed lift-off, although a "technical flight" of one foot was claimed for *Cygnet III*. (The *Oionos* and *Cygnet III* were built by the Canadian Aerodrome Company, a short-lived venture set up by Baldwin, McCurdy, and Bell when the A.E.A. ended, in the hopes of manufacturing aircraft for the Canadian government.) Bell gave up, though not on flight itself; he and Casey Baldwin began work on development of the hydrofoil, the boat that actually flies.

Tetrahedral planes were not to be, but tetrahedral structures were. Today space frames cross rivers, span roofs, and in general do all that Mabel Bell and her consultants thought they would, although few people, including the designers who rediscovered the concept, realize the idea was originally Bell's. Says the space frame's great popularizer, Buckminster Fuller, "I'd been at what I discovered possibly fifteen years before somebody said, 'Didn't you know Alexander Graham Bell did it?'"

Glenn Curtiss with the Curtiss II engine he brought to the Beinn Bhreagh laboratory for demonstration in July 1907.

Taken 1904 hot once
Dev. 1904 hot glater.

Above:
Inspecting an engine-equipped kite are Bell, members of his family, and some of his assistants. (1907)

Left:
Thomas Selfridge and friends with the Bells in the launch. (Douglas McCurdy, 1907)

Opposite page:
The giant *Cygnet,* built of 3,400 tetrahedral cells and designed to carry a man and engine, aboard a tow raft. (Douglas McCurdy, 1907)

The *Blue Hill* towing the *Cygnet*
with Selfridge aboard. (John Michael McNeil, December 6, 1907)

The *Silver Dart,* fourth plane of the
A.E.A., being readied for takeoff.
(1909)

View of the *Red Wing,* pioneer
craft of the A.E.A., showing the
position of the Curtiss V-8 forty-
horsepower air-cooled engine and
the construction of the wings, rud-
der, and stabilizer. It crashed on
its second flight, with Casey Baldwin as pilot. (He was uninjured.)
(1908)

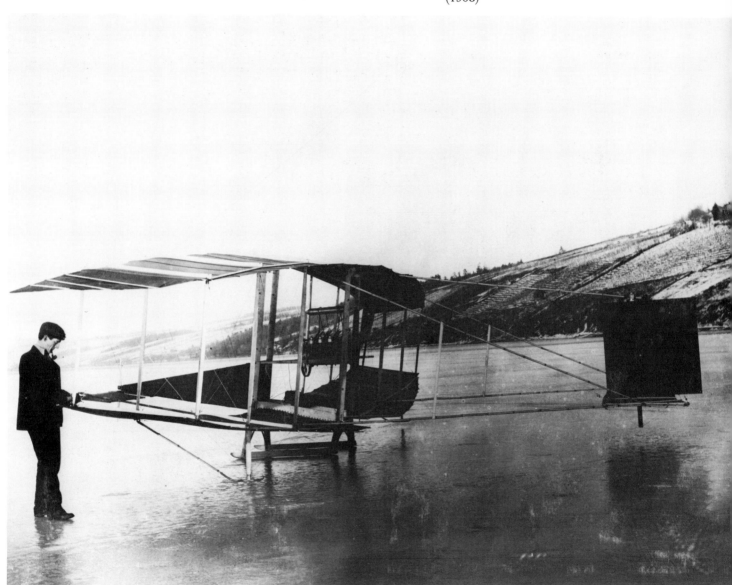

Half-size model of Bell's tetrahedral triplane *Oionos*. It had two
layers of cells mounted in opposite
directions separating three horizontal wings. In 1910 it was tested un-
successfully. (John Michael
McNeil, 1909)

The *Cygnet II,* 1909. Despite Douglas McCurdy's efforts as pilot, it never achieved lift-off.

The *White Wing* after crashing with Douglas McCurdy as pilot during its fourth flight, in May 1908. The plane was equipped with a tricycle undercarriage for land takeoffs and had ailerons on the wings, both aviation firsts in North America.

The Hydrofoil Years

"Mr. Baldwin is designing another boat from which he and Alec expect wonderful things," wrote Mabel Bell in August of 1908. In fact the boat, built during the summer of the A.E.A.'s existence, was designed in the hopes of its becoming an airplane. The aim of its designers was that it should rise up out of the water on hydrofoils and then take off and fly. This failed to happen, and so the *Dhonnas Beag*—Gaelic for "little devil" and dubbed thus by a Beinn Bhreagh workman, according to C. R. Roseberry in his *Glenn Curtiss: Pioneer of Flight*—became the first Bell-Baldwin hydrofoil model to move over the water under its own power.

At least seven years earlier, as a result of his investigations into aerial takeoff, Bell had begun to think in the direction of hydrofoils—boats with ladders of slanted blades attached to their hulls on which they rise above the resistance of the water.

Bell had recorded in his notes as early as September 2, 1901: "Whatever resistance the water may offer to a body going through it at a certain velocity—THE AIR WOULD OFFER LESS RESISTANCE. If, therefore, with increase of speed the boat or vessel could be elevated more and more out of the water so that the chief part of the resistance should be the air, would not the engine power be more economically utilised under such circumstances? Would not, for example, torpedo boat destroyers be able to go at greater speed with the same engine power than they do now if they were so constructed above as to utilise the resistance of the air to lift them—at least partially out of the water?"

These thoughts stayed in his mind. The idea was not new: back in 1861 a hydrofoil boat had been tested under tow in England and in the early 1900s William E. Meacham in the United States and Enrico Forlanini in Italy had pioneered hydrofoil development. (Bell was later to buy their patents.) "I consider the invention of the hydroplane as the most significant of recent years," he wrote in 1906.

Tests with the *Query*, a second model, were made in 1909. Then, during a world tour that lasted from 1910 to 1911 and on which the Baldwins accompanied the Bells, the entire party visited

Descending the rustic stairway to the Beinn Bhreagh dock. (Gilbert Grosvenor)

Forlanini, where both Bell and Casey Baldwin rode Forlanini's hydrofoil on Lake Maggiore at what Mabel Bell estimated was express-train speed—forty-five miles an hour.

As soon as the Bells returned to Canada in the summer of 1911, work on a new hydrofoil began. From that date on until the outbreak of World War I, the Beinn Bhreagh workshops constructed and refined hydrofoil models to Baldwin's designs: the HD-1, which when rebuilt became the HD-2, the HD-3, and an unsatisfactory hydrofoil sailboat. (The letters "HD" stand for "hydrodrome," for in both hydrofoils and flying machines Bell was faithful to the terminology of his friend, the ill-fated pioneer Samuel Pierpont Langley, who called his test models "aerodromes," from the Greek words *aero dromos,* "air runner." Bell and his A.E.A. associates sometimes referred to their planes as "dromes" and talked of "droming" Baddeck Bay.)

The *Dhonnas Beag,* the first Bell-Baldwin hydrofoil to travel under its own power. (1908)

137

On his return from the 1911 tour Baldwin became manager of the estate and the laboratory. Bell, then sixty-four, moved his office to leave the lab to Casey. "He transferred up to the kite house by the kite field where they had the *Frost King* stored when they were using it," says Mayme Morrison Brown, recalling the move. "It was more quiet there. It was a great big building. They had used it as a hangar but they renovated and the room was all fixed up with his old rolltop desk, very ancient, and all scarred and burned with his pipes and cluttered with his tobacco and everything." (According to Freddie Pinaud, who had heard it from his father, one of Bell's favorite sayings was, "There is no thinking without smoking.")

Although about to enter the last decade of his life, Bell, in his study at the Point House, continued his habit of working till the small hours. The Beinn Bhreagh household, under Mabel's direction, continued to supply perfect backup services, of course, although the odd slipup is recorded. "You know I was up all night preparing instructions for Mr. McNeil relating to the apparatus to measure the lift and drift of hydroplanes," Bell wrote in a note left for Mabel on such an occasion. "I wrote two notes to him fully illustrated by diagrams and enclosed with them the rough models he had made and put them on the kitchen table at daybreak with a note to Charles telling him to send them down to Mr. McNeil at the laboratory. . . . Charles reports the cook found them this morning and thought someone was trying to play a joke upon her and put them in the stove. Please make a ROW. . . ."

Unlike various assistants and associates who worked with Bell on the telephone and the graphophone and shared in his successes, Hector P. McNeil, perhaps the most inventive of the Beinn Bhreagh laboratory workers upon whom Bell relied, was to end his life not much richer than he had started. The rewards that might have accrued today to a holder of a joint patent on a universal connector did not materialize. McNeil died blind. When his eyesight failed, Bell sent him to specialists in Boston but nothing could be done. His eyes had been ruined, it is said in Baddeck, by a doctor who had given him the wrong drops.

Domestically, these later years in which his interests seemed to focus on the water were good years for Bell. Perhaps he missed the lively collaboration he had enjoyed during the lifetime of the A.E.A.—although frictions had erupted among "the boys"— but he had a compatible associate in Casey Baldwin and also found great pleasure in the frequent company of his growing grandchildren, in whose education and well-being both he and Mabel had enormous interest. "Send me some of the latest sayings of Graham and Barbara," he would write. Or, "Wish Elsie and Daisy and all

The hydrofoil *Query* under tow on Baddeck Bay. (John Michael McNeil, 1909)

the children could be here in this beautifully cool, bracing air and out of the 'atmosphere of doctors.' Doctors are all very well in emergencies, but . . ."

The Bells and their daughter, Daisy Fairchild were supporters of the progressive theories of education that were becoming current. In the summer of 1913 a Montessori class for the grandchildren was held in a Beinn Bhreagh warehouse, and in autumn of the same year Mabel sponsored the first Montessori school in Washington in her own house. Frequently the new theories paralleled Bell's own beliefs regarding the way knowledge is best absorbed. As Melville Grosvenor, his eldest grandchild, grew up, Bell began to devise simple scientific experiments to intrigue him and the other grandchildren.

From my house on Crescent Grove I can look across the bay to the Beinn Bhreagh point, where the great bald-headed eagles circle against the trees, and see Bell's old kite house. These summers it is occupied once again by Daisy's daughter Barbara Fairchild Muller, one of the younger grandchildren, and her husband, Leonard. "We were all influenced by the scientific way of thinking," she told me. "Of course, I was pretty young . . . it was for and with my brother Graham and my cousin Melville that he set up the experiments to illustrate various principles of physics. . . . The only one I remember clearly is to have been asked to fill a bottle with very hot water and then to cork the bottle. Time after time when we later checked the bottle—cool—it was not full and we were told to repeat, refill, recork, recheck. Still, the bottle never stayed full when it cooled off. Great mystery for a six- or seven-year-old!"

A scientific exhibit that made a vivid impression on all the grandchildren, Barbara Muller recalls, was the array of unborn lambs, pickled in alcohol, that lined the shelves of Bell's sheep house. She is intrigued by the suggestion that long before there was general interest in the matter her grandfather worked on the problems of birth control. Could these bottled specimens, she wonders, have had an effect on local rumor and led to the speculation that Bell did research in this field? For their part, the grandchildren found the exhibit of absorbing interest. "[The lambs] started from about a quarter of an inch all the way up to about four inches long. We used to go up and gawk. Oh, we were too young to find them upsetting. We thought it very interesting to know what baby lambs looked like before they were born."

A witness to life at Beinn Bhreagh in the years 1917 to 1920 was the young Edith (Polly) MacMechan Dobson, daughter of Archibald MacMechan, a Dalhousie University professor and author of *There Go the Ships* and *The Halifax Disaster*. Like so many who worked for the Bells, Polly MacMechan found her life irrevocably changed by her summertime association with the family. In 1917 she was nineteen, a young girl "full of life" and an obvious favorite, remembers Norman Bethune, the doctor's son who worked over at Beinn Bhreagh then. Subsequently she toured the world with her naval husband and bore twin daughters in Australia. She lives today in a Halifax apartment. Visitors there swiftly succumb to the charm—a mix of consideration and verve—that must have made her a formidable organizer of Beinn Bhreagh activities (charades, farmers' banquets, French babies relief) and a knockout as the admiral's lady she eventually became. I sat with her, eating lobster-paste sandwiches ("You've had a plastic lunch on the plane") while she evoked the secluded but productive life of the

Opposite page
Above:
An early hydrofoil at the launching wharf, with the boat sheds in the background. (Notman Studios, 1912–1916)
Below:
Bell and Hector P. McNeil with hydrofoil models, 1912.

141

Bells during and immediately after World War I, a period when spirits ran high but a certain formality prevailed—"We always seemed to be wearing those big hats at picnics!"

"Casey Baldwin was one of Mr. Bell's young men," she explained. "Mr. Bell loved young men—having them about him—and after the Aerial Experimental Association, Casey stayed on doing experiments with Mr. Bell. As a wedding present Mr. and Mrs. Bell gave Casey and Kathleen, a second cousin of my mother's, a bungalow on the Beinn Bhreagh property. In 1916 I had just got out of school in England and Kathleen was up in Halifax for fun—going to parties—and she said, 'Wouldn't you like to come down to Baddeck and visit us in the summer?' Well, I just adored it . . . all the sailing . . . it was the kind of life I loved

The Bells' Grosvenor grandchildren: Gertrude, Carol, Melville, Lilian, Alexander, and Mabel, about 1914.

. . . and of course I saw a lot of the Bells that summer. Mrs. Bell wrote me in February [1917] saying would I consider coming as her secretary? Gretchen Schmitt had been her secretary, but the Bells were starting a boat-building program for the Canadian Navy . . . small boats, the plant was quite small . . . and they were going to have girls working in it and were turning their original house on the property into a residence for them. Gretchen was going to take charge. She was very conscious of her German name, and was determined to do something for the good of the war. She was Gretchen Anton Smith by then; she had changed her name by deed of poll.

"I didn't know anything about being a secretary . . . it was really the '14–'18 war that started careers for girls . . . and I was awfully afraid I wasn't going to be able to do it. But Mrs. Bell was very helpful and there was nothing formal about it. Mrs. Bell was in complete charge of the household. I arranged the picnics and all the comings and goings.

"The only thing I absolutely had to do was to be ready for Mr. Bell at eleven o'clock to take notes. The routine was that he used to have breakfast upstairs in his study and then get up. From eleven to twelve I'd write down in longhand everything that had happened—if somebody had arrived to stay or somebody had gone, who came to dinner the night before. It was like a diary. I took the domestic things; there were two facets, so to speak. At the office it was all technical, and his secretary Catherine MacKenzie took that. You see Casey's handwriting quite often, too, and Kathleen's and maybe Mr. Byrnes', the estate manager. Mr. Bell used to call them in and get them to put down their reports in the book. And there are occasional notes in shorthand. Those are Mr. Bell's secrets. He had his own private shorthand,* which nobody could translate. Something he made up himself, I think. Top secret!

"Those two young men who came down two or three years ago to ask questions for the Baddeck Museum said how would I like it if they photostated every page of the Home Notes where I was mentioned. Well, I said that would be the greatest fun. It's just like looking into another life. I go back and say I can't believe that happened. And then of course it brings a picture to my mind. Isn't the formality charming: in the family Mr. Bell did call me Polly, but in the notes I'm Miss MacMechan."

---

* Probably the system of shorthand developed by Alexander Melville Bell from the notation system for Visible Speech, his universally applicable phonetic alphabet.

The *Elsie,* launched from Bell's boatyard in 1919, on the Bras d'Or. (Gilbert Grosvenor)

In the Beinn Bhreagh Home Notes of February 20, 1920, I found the following exchange:

Mr. Bell: I want Miss MacMechan to promise to do something for me that will not involve physical or mental exertion. What do you say, Miss MacMechan?

Miss MacMechan: I have a guilty feeling that I know what Mr. Bell is going to ask, but I promise.

Mr. Bell: Follow the instructions of the Sydney Board of Health regarding preparedness to meet an attack of flu—by going to bed and resting quietly. Miss MacMechan has caught cold and is evidently feeling miserably this morning.

Bell's routine rarely varied, Polly discovered. "Mr. Bell's lunch used to come up on a tray and he'd finish dressing and come down and John was always there with the horses and very often Mrs. Bell used to drive with him down to the office.

"When I arrived, the hydrofoil, the HD-4, was being built in the sheds on the Beinn Bhreagh property below the bungalow. Casey did much of the supervising. Mr. Bell was getting to be a pretty old man then . . . not all that old, but he was heavy and getting round about the sheds was not too easy. Casey oversaw it. If Mr. Bell had an idea, he'd very often sketch it, and then if it was going to be made in the workshop, Casey used to draw it to scale and make it more exact.

"Mrs. Bell used to go down to meet him, too. She'd send John home with the horses, and they'd walk the last half mile home along the upper level road, which was all downhill.

"Mrs. Bell always wanted him to take more exercise, and he wasn't keen on doing it! He used to try to get out of it, although he loved swimming. There were stories that before my time he used to go down about midnight and get into the water and light a cigar and float about the lake with his hands behind his head. The neighbors thought that was quite something!

"It was a lovely household to be in; Mrs. Bell was a genius at running a big household. Now the grandchildren have built houses all over the property, but then two sets of grandchildren arrived to stay at the Point. There were five or six Grosvenors and three Fairchilds with all the things they wanted to do. And all the other relations and visitors all summer long. The Bells were more than hospitable!

"As you know, Mrs. Bell was completely deaf. It came from scarlet fever when she was just a little thing. She had a perfectly wonderful mind and it was bad luck. I did as I was told, but a lot of people couldn't make her understand. She said, 'People make faces at me; just *talk* to me.' People would mouth at her, and that

145

was defeating for her. Of course, you had to turn your face towards her . . . never speak with your head turned away. The grandchildren realized from the time they learned to talk. As little things they would climb on her lap and talk right to her."

In adult life the grandchildren have often attested that they knew their grandmother was a remarkable person. But they never seemed to think of her as handicapped. They followed their grandfather's example and took her affliction as a mtter of course. In their younger years he kept them up to the mark. At family mealtimes—sometimes there would be sixteen or seventeen at the table—the grandchildren were never allowed to chatter privately among themselves. Bell would interrupt and say, "You must tell your grandmother." Speaking to Joan Marshall, a broadcaster who interviewed a number of Bell grandchildren for a Canadian Broadcasting Corporation program, Elsie's daughter Lilian Grosvenor Jones said, "It always made a tremendous impression on me . . . the *theme*, it always seemed to me as a child . . . the sound and the silence. He was always trying to re-create sound for her and she was always trying to understand that sound. . . . She couldn't remember sound. And she wrote once that she imagined it was something like the sound of humming of the bees.

"And always when we would walk with them, he was always telling her the sound he heard . . . a cow bell or whatever it was."

On another occasion Barbara Fairchild Muller also remarked on how little aware she was as a child of her grandmother's deafness. "It took me a long time to know that my grandmother was deaf. We heard the servants talking and there were certain pronunciations of words—she would say 'cup-board' rather than 'cubbord'—and there was one experience with charades. She was great for charades, and once I was supposed to be something or other with curls and my hair of course was straight as a board. She was very annoyed with the maid because she had said, 'Iron them, iron them,' and they took me out and put my head on the ironing board and ironed each curl. You know what they came out like, and of course she had meant to say to use tongs! I can see myself—I must have been about nine or ten—with my head on the ironing board, having my curls ironed.

"She had a certain inflection in her voice. Deaf people do, although I have known deaf people in my life who had absolutely none. In teaching the hard of hearing they seem to be regressing towards sign language. We feel very badly that they are going back to it. There was only one time I knew Grandmama to use sign language. When we were children each one of us (when we were younger) slept out on the porch with them. I would hear her voice and then silence and then her voice and silence. He was

A granddaughter riding sidesaddle, about 1914.

146

Lilian, Mabel, and Gertrude Grosvenor followed by their pet goat. (Gilbert Grosvenor, 1914)

Mabel Bell at her desk.

spelling into her hand and she was answering. I never saw Grandmama or Grandpapa use sign language. Never. Only lip reading.
We all got pretty good at it. We really did."

"Mrs. Bell was a very wealthy woman," Polly MacMechan
Dobson continued. "The Hubbards were people of great means; as
you know, it was Mrs. Bell's father who really pushed Mr. Bell
into getting the telephone on the market. If you read the books,
you see that Bell did get a substantial sum from the telephone but
the stock he had was infinitesimal. The dividend was paid just
about the time of my birthday in November and he always gave it
to me as a present; the dividend was twenty-five dollars. But Mr.
Bell was very wise . . . he didn't want to be bothered with petty
cash and money and bills and Mrs. Bell was more than willing. I
was Mrs. Bell's secretary, so I paid the bills. That was fun, too—a
great eye-opener for me as to what real money can do.

"The Bells brought everyone to Baddeck—they discovered it.
Everyone beat a path to their door. There were no crowned heads
in my time, and Helen Keller and the missionary Wilfred Grenfell
were also earlier, but the lieutenant governor of Nova Scotia arrived one year and that was quite a to-do. He'd forgotten his dinner trousers—they'd never been packed. When she entertained,
Mrs. Bell often gave fancy-dress balls. They were great levelers,
though I didn't realize it at the time. But Mrs. Bell was extremely
sensitive, and her Baddeck friends were often poor. Her Washington friends were rich.

"Getting to Baddeck was pretty frightful. You got off the train from Halifax at six-thirty in the morning and you sat on the platform at Iona until eight-thirty, when the *Blue Hill* steamed over from Baddeck, and about nine you got aboard and went back with it. If you were visiting the Bells, of course, they had lots of boats. But there's a story—it dates from before my time—about two people from Washington or Boston arriving early Sunday morning and asking the stationmaster at Iona to telephone the Point to say they were there. But the stationmaster wouldn't use the phone on Sunday. The Americans offered him anything—lots of money—and simply couldn't understand how anyone could have principles so strong . . . or be so pigheaded! They just had to sit there grilling on the Iona dock.

"But even in those days there was quite an American colony at Baddeck. Because of the Bells. Miss Augusta and Miss Caroline McCurdy, Mrs. Bell's cousins, were part of it. Miss Augusta could hear a little—you had to shout at her. . . . Miss Caroline couldn't hear at all—you had to write to her. You'd start, and she would get the sentence and finish it. Playing bridge with them was something. We did it all by signs—hearts, a hand over the heart; diamonds, a hand on the ring finger.

"Mrs. Bell's was the age of letter writing. People had time . . . in spite of the telephone! She had quite a vast correspondence and used to spend a good deal of time at her desk in the morning. And she wrote little sketches for acting. . . . One play she wrote was about the Cape North cable connection . . . the only cable connection then between America and overseas. We were always putting on charades and amateur theatricals in Baddeck to raise money for the war effort. And she was always getting things started . . . the Baddeck library was one of her projects . . . and the Young Ladies' Club.

"Mrs. Bell was a perfectly wonderful grandmother. She adored her grandchildren and really enjoyed them. She didn't want them to have holiday tasks. It was such a lovely life; there was practically nowhere that any harm could come to them. So they swam and they picnicked and they all did their thing. Graham Fairchild was always collecting snakes and dissecting them. He was encouraged to do so. Of course, Mrs. Bell had been absolutely taken up with Madame Montessori when she first met her and backed the first Montessori school in Washington. The Fairchild grandchildren were all Montessori children and Carol was, too, although I think the other Grosvenors were beyond it by the time she got started. So we went on the principle that nobody must do anything for the children; they must do everything for themselves. Sometimes the results weren't too good. The children

Edith (Polly) MacMechan Dobson, Mabel's secretary from 1917 to 1920, when she was about twenty-two.

J. D. Smith about 1919 with Winifred McNeil, principal of Red Head's one-room schoolhouse, and his mother, Margaret Ann Smith (right). Employees at Beinn Bhreagh often boarded at the estate's farm with the Smiths.

bathed themselves and washed their hair and did everything. But people began to notice that one of the little girls was scratching her head tremendously. The child's head was full of lice! It was a terrible time for the child—she had to be soaked in kerosene and her head tied up. There were two young men visiting that summer, and the child told them she had cooties in her head. They called her 'the Cootie Queen.' They were very self-sufficient children.

"Before dinner, with the younger children around, Mr. Bell used to play the piano which was in the hall. They were all pretty musical, and the younger children used to sing and march around to the tune of 'Nicodemus the slave was of African birth and bought for a bag full of gold.' The chorus was 'The good time coming is nearly here . . . it's a long, long time on the way! So come tell Elijah to hurry up Pop, and we'll wake Nicodemus today!' One of the children would be on the sofa pretending to be asleep and the others would march around singing while their grandfather played. Then to wake Nicodemus they'd get hold of the one who was supposed to be sleeping. . . . It was very enchanting and they all enjoyed it."

The grandchildren remember lots of singing. Says Lilian Grosvenor Jones, "We did a lot of spirituals, Scotch songs, and Gilbert and Sullivan . . . 'Tit Willow,' 'I'm Going to Marry Yum-Yum.'"

"I think it was Sunday night that we always had the sings. Grandmama would put her hand upon the piano and would sing along with us," Barbara Fairchild Muller recalls. The old songs from the land of Bell's birth apparently were the favorites. "You'd know he was Scots," remembers Mayme Morrison Brown. "You could hear 'Annie Laurie' all over the house. He could really bang it."

Polly MacMechan Dobson also recalls the musical efforts. "There were often charades and amateur theatricals and reading aloud. A lot of singing. That's another thing . . . I am absolutely tone-deaf, and I was always told at school to stop singing because I put the girl next to me off. Mr. Bell was determined that it didn't matter; he worked with me. He was so interested in everything to do with ears and tones and how you could teach people without them having any music in them. And I remember him sitting at the piano and getting me to try 'Love's Old Sweet Song' over and over again. And eventually he got me to keep the tune. It didn't stick, though.

"I think Mr. Bell's greatest characteristic was that he was a born teacher . . . he loved teaching. There are ways and ways of teaching, and some of them are very boring, but not with Mr.

Bell. He took so much trouble and interest with his grandchildren. In fact, his daughters used to say that the grandchildren had the best of him. When they were children it was 'Don't interfere with Papa; don't disturb him!' He was a genius at work. But by the time the grandchildren came along he was at their disposal.

"After dinner Mr. Bell really liked conversation. Very often the Baldwins came up for dinner, and Mr. Bell and Casey used to retire to the study shortly after. He and Casey would be up until two or three in the morning. Neither he nor Casey was an early riser. Mrs. Bell would have preferred otherwise, but she knew that was his pattern and the way he liked to work, and of course she had the greatest respect for his brain. They'd get interested in something they were thinking of trying; Casey would draw plans and they would talk and talk.

"It was the HD-4 that interested them most while I was there."

With the outbreak of World War I, Bell and Baldwin's work on hydrofoils halted. Bell's sympathies were with the British, but since his own country was not at war, he confined the production of the Beinn Bhreagh laboratory and boatyard to the construction of lifeboats for the Canadian Department of Naval Services. In 1917, when American involvement was certain, he turned again to the hydrofoil, convinced of its important military significance.

I hadn't been in Baddeck more than a few hours when I drove into Bethune's Garage and met Norman Bethune, who had once, I later learned, spent a dusty summer working on the famous "cigar boat." Like others in Baddeck, Norman Bethune succumbed to the lure of the mechanical age. But it was cars rather than aircraft or hydrofoils that took his interest, and Bethune's Garage—where they always wash the windshield—was Baddeck's first gas station, "except," says Mr. Bethune, "for the pump on the wharf."

Norman Bethune knew the Bells from his earliest childhood. "Mrs. Bell often came with the horses and the buckboard to pick up my mother," he recalls. During the kite experiments, an older brother, Roderick (Rory), and John Michael McNeil, the son of Hector P. NcNeil, Bell's assistant, went with Bell to Washington, D.C. for a winter. "Rory did nothing but fly kites and John Michael did nothing but take pictures."

One of Norman Bethune's first jobs (at the height of the 1914–1918 war, when he was sixteen) was to drive Charles Martin, a Washington photographer, around Cape Breton as he took photographs for a *National Geographic* article. Off North Ingonish, Martin hired a boat so that he could photograph the coast. On his return Martin found himself arrested. "They thought he was a spy.

They took him up to Sheriff Doucet and the sheriff took him up to his house. Charlie wrote two, three telegrams, and I was sent to buy some oranges and a bottle. Nothing much happened for the afternoon. Then the messages began to arrive. There were dozens, and I'm sure there was one from the president of the United States."

A summer or two later Norman Bethune was employed at Beinn Bhreagh to work on the HD-4. "The hydrofoil—the cigar—was in the shed at the end of the large shop where they were building the lifeboats. They had it in the water, and there was a man from the United States Navy who was installing the motors. I was grinding the bevel on the hydrofoils. Oh, grind all day long, day after day. They came flat pieces of metal in different widths—two inches, three inches, and six inches wide and I suppose half an inch or three-eighths of an inch thick. There were square edges on them and we'd cut them off at a slant. I spent weeks on the grinding of the bevel. Boring? No, it wasn't at the time. Because there was enough to make it interesting. You had to make sure you didn't grind too deeply in one spot. And you'd run the pattern along to make sure the angle was the same. They were ground on an emery wheel. They had a generator—partly run by water, but they helped it out with a gas engine. I didn't assemble, but they were welded into struts to rise up on the water."

One afternoon Norman Bethune assisted Bell as he experimented with converting his telephonic medical probe (hastily invented in 1881 in an effort to locate the assassin's bullet lodged in the body of President Garfield and thus possibly save his life) into an underwater metal detector that might recover a load of metal fittings which had fallen off the Beinn Bhreagh scow.

"At the same time the cigar was going on, they were building lifeboats," Norman Bethune remembered. "One day Mr. Pinaud, the manager of the boatyard, told me Mr. Bell was coming down and I was to go to the pond near the warehouse. Mr. Bell was there with the coachman, John MacDermid, and the span of horses, and MacDermid was unloading some batteries and sort of a telephone and some wire. Dr. Bell called me by name, Bethune, because he and my father had been friends. He told me he had some work for me to do. This wire had a steel rod at the end of it, about six feet long and about as big around as my finger, and he told me to go out into the pond to wade about, and to touch things on the bottom with the rod. He was listening with the telephone, and when I touched anything he asked me to bend down and pick it up. It might be an empty bottle or a rusty plate. I just had sneakers on and my trousers rolled up above the knee.

"The purpose was . . . two weeks before, they had been trans-

Right:
Keeping cool under the hose.
Below:
Bobby and Betty, children of
Casey and Kathleen Baldwin, out
for a row. (About 1918–1919)

154

porting some galvanized fittings that had come by rail for the lifeboats on their own scow. Many tons of these fittings. There was a sea running that day and as they turned from the channel into the wharf, the scow lurched and the fittings slithered to one side. The next wave that came, everything slid off. Tons and tons of this valuable metal . . . iron bars, eight to ten feet long.

"It's fairly deep out in the channel, and the idea was they might locate those bars by their sound and grapple for them.

"I suppose we were there two hours. I had one of those bars at a certain position near the shore, and he'd ask me to go and touch it once in a while so he could distinguish it by the noise it made. He was holding a telephone receiver and a wire in his other hand, and he'd move along the shore—I thought at the time it was mostly to keep in the shade!* But he got me to take my time rubbing things. He was interested—he seemed bouncy to me. His genius? Curiosity! And intelligence, of course. He was curious about everything. Even the most commonplace thing, he'd inquire into it.

"With the hot summer, and with all the dust from this grinding, I didn't like the job on the cigar too much, so I left the first of July. I never saw the cigar traveling. I went down to Sydney and drove a car for the steel company for six months and then opened the garage here in Baddeck.

"There are just three fellows alive now who worked on the HD-4: myself; Douglas Fraser, who took over the grinding after I left (he told me the other day he can still taste the dust from the emery); and Murdoch Stewart."

Sixteen-year-old Norman Bethune acting up for the camera.

---

* According to J. H. Parkin in *Bell and Baldwin,* with the aid of the telephone detector, most of the metal fittings were eventually recovered.

"There are few things in the life of a child," David Fairchild wrote beside this picture, "that can compare with a small bridge from which you can look down into the stream below and with some kind of a net catch the water animals there." Daisy Bell Fairchild with Barbara and Graham Fairchild. (David Fairchild, about 1911)

Women workers at Beinn Bhreagh
during World War I. (Charles
Martin, 1918)

Out for a ride. Bell gives family and friends a send-off. (Charles Martin, 1918)

Casey Baldwin leans on the cock-
pit of the Bell-Baldwin hydrofoil
HD-4. (Gilbert Grosvenor)

Riding the HD-4

One night in about 1925 Murdoch Stewart, then a young apprentice accountant, was seated in a movie house in Sydney, Nova Scotia, watching some sports shorts. Suddenly he turned to his friend in the next seat and said, "That's me you're looking at!"

"A lot of sports events were shown," he remembers, "and then suddenly there was a picture of the HD-4 the day we set the record. Just a picture of the machine and me." The date was September 9, 1919, and for many years the HD-4, the craft Bell and Baldwin timed that day, was the fastest ship in the world.

Now a retired accountant, Murdoch Stewart lives on a Sydney side street with his wife, Helen. In 1918, just out of school, to earn some money he went to work for the summer at Beinn Bhreagh, where his father, William Stewart, was chief carpenter. Dan Stewart, Murdoch's brother, says, "They were looking for someone young and active to go out on the HD-4. Murdoch was ideal for it."

"At Dr. Bell's I did work around motors," explains Murdoch Stewart. "They used to come kind of natural to me. I read in a magazine not long ago that some people have the power to make machines operate more efficiently just by some inner force. There was a motor there in the machine shop that they always had trouble with and I got the machine working just as good as it could. The strange thing was sometimes I'd get it going like lightning without going near it; just by looking at it. The foreman came along one day and the motor seemed to be going extraordinarily fast and he said, 'I don't know what the heck's the matter with that Stewart!'

"Dr. Bell sent for me and he said something about needing somebody active to go out on the boat and I believe he said something about there being some risk."

"It was one of the world's inventions," comments Murdoch's wife, Helen, "and Murdoch is the only living human being who was on it."*

Murdoch Stewart at twenty-two.

* The only crew member still alive.

The HD-4 leaving the boatshed.
The craft was launched from a
cradle fitted on a track running
into the water. (Gilbert Grosvenor)

Murdoch himself told me: "At first we didn't know what the machine was capable of doing. Nobody knew. You know what the design was like? She had those wings. The HD-4 was sixty feet long with this big platform on both sides shaped up in the front and lower behind like the wings of an airplane. There was a lot of airlift to those things and there was airlift from the hydros. So the chap who was with me, an older man called Bill MacDonald from Baddeck Bay, mentioned one day that he was kind of concerned that if the thing got going too fast, it might lift off. I didn't think there was much danger of that. I wasn't worrying about it. In fact, all I was thinking about was the thrill of getting out on her, hoping she'd go fast.

"But after the first couple of flights, when we got back, I couldn't hear the other fellow talking. There were two Liberty airplane motors on the HD-4 and it took five hundred horsepower to drive her. When you were in between those two engines it was pretty noisy, so we got something to plug our ears and we were all right after that.

"The only thing I really minded was getting the hail in my face. That didn't happen too often because we only got the spray at seventy miles an hour. Then it was like being out in a hailstorm and sometimes we'd have to put our hands up.

"The first run I was on didn't amount to anything . . . we went about thirty miles an hour. Every time they made tests they'd come back and reset the hydrofoils.

"The adjustment of the hydros was the important thing. There were hydros made of welded steel under the ship but a few feet above these were big long wooden hydros, probably about eight or nine inches wide, that went from one side of the ship to the other so that when she started picking up speed they kind of raised her up off the water until the metal hydros took over.

"The metal hydros could be adjusted forward or backward so the pitch was changed. Even one inch or two inches on the tilt of the hydros made a tremendous difference to the pitch. Getting the right angle before launching took a lot of experience. It took a good many trial runs to actually get the most efficient angle.

"The hydrofoil principle is quite simple . . . a stone will skim over the water; it gets on angle and it lifts up. You often see a stone jumping up. It's the same thing.

"The whole purpose was to build a ship for the navy. Casey Baldwin thought the ship could be a submarine chaser. Because of its speed and because on the surface of the water it wouldn't be so susceptible to torpedoes. They'd go under it.

"The HD-4 wasn't something that happened suddenly. Dr. Bell experimented with the principle for years. Probably he experimented with hydrofoils for takeoff when he was working with kites. It would have been a practical use for them. Then he used to build little boats, maybe thirty feet long, and put hydros under them and measure the resistance to the water.

"Casey Baldwin was the principal designer. You see, Dr. Bell knew a lot about angles and that sort of thing, but Dr. Bell wasn't an engineer; Casey was. It was a good team. All the experience Dr. Bell gained through his models he passed on to Casey and Casey Baldwin was a very clever man.

"Casey was always on the HD-4; he steered the ship. Dr. Bell had his picture taken aboard, but we were tied up at the wharf. I'm there with a cap on. They had some photographers down from New York and were taking pictures of Dr. Bell and the ship. I had this cap on and of course our clothes were covered with grease, and I felt a little self-conscious and began to take it off. Dr. Bell said, 'Lad, don't change; leave it on.'

"He was rather eccentric like all of those fellows. Grumpy? Could be. But he was never cross at any of the men. When he looked at you, he looked right through you, trying to figure out what made you work. Quite often he'd entertain the staff. There'd be general discussion . . . very informal. Dinner was the main event, and quite elaborate, with about twenty or thirty there. I remember one time after most had gone home there were a few who stayed around. There were some drinks and Dr. Bell had a few drinks and played the piano. We started to sing 'Auld Lang Syne.' But he played it so often! He was feeling good. He didn't want to go home. Finally someone came down looking for him. His people were getting worried about him.

"On the HD-4 I had various duties. We had to keep the motors in check, and that meant that when we came in from a run we had to drain the oil off. And every time we went out, the motors had to be refilled with fresh oil. They had to be heated in order to start the machine up. Sometimes it took half or three-quarters of an hour to do that. Originally we had to start them with our hands and that was kind of dangerous, but then they got compressed air tanks. They had a compressed air motor on the machine. You let the air into the motor and when the pilots were on, they'd start. So that was quite simple.

"Launching the ship was kind of tricky and so especially was getting her in after a run. The first time I ever saw the HD-4 she was in the shed. She was on a cradle which fitted under the ship and the cradle was on a railway running into the water. The railway was on an incline so the ship went into the water by its own momentum—with a little push sometimes! But getting her back in was the problem! It was difficult to get her in exactly the right position on the cradle so she would balance. That was my responsibility. I used to stand on the forward deck and there was a big post . . . a two-by-four or something like that was attached to the cradle and sticking out of the water. This post was coming towards you, and when it was close enough you grabbed ahold of it and kind of tried to force the boat into position. Then they'd pull her in with an engine. Oh, she was heavy at times . . . she weighed ten thousand pounds . . . but she was easy to maneuver. It was a little tricky at times, but I never had too much trouble.

"Local people got quite familiar with watching this machine in the water. One day Casey Baldwin decided to take the HD-4 to Sydney. I went over in the morning not knowing that we were going. But Casey was all ready with two or three cases of port aboard. We started out and everything was going fine. If nothing had happened, at sixty miles an hour I'd say we'd have been at Sydney in an hour easy. We came around Beinn Bhreagh and Dr. Bell's home. You could see everybody running down towards the

Bell with grandson Melville about 1920.

163

The HD-4 at the Beinn Bhreagh
wharf. (Gilbert Grosvenor)

shore. There was a tremendous noise. Everybody heard it and wondered what was happening.

"We made good headway to the entrance to Big Bras d'Or. There the sea was on the roar from the ocean. We saw a big roar coming and Casey slowed up; he was afraid to keep his speed. As he slowed, a big breaker came and smashed the wooden lift they used to start her up out of the water. She settled down in the water and you couldn't start her up again; the wooden hydro was broken. So we had to be towed back to Baddeck; we never got to Sydney. Even if I wasn't equipped for the visit . . . I'd my old cap on with all the grease . . . I was disappointed.

"The day she made the record was September 9, 1919. Quite early in the summer we began with the runs and she was out twelve or fifteen times. Of course, you couldn't take this machine out in any kind of water. She wasn't built to go in rough seas, and you don't find too many summer days when it's perfectly calm. That's probably why it took so long to get her to maximum speed.

"Personally I was a little dubious about her efficiency as a submarine chaser . . . because she wanted calm waters. For instance, in the ocean you get thirty- to forty-foot waves, and when you're traveling 60 or 70 miles an hour you have to have a very, very strong structure underneath to withstand the pressure of those waves at that speed.

"To clock her they measured off the distance of a mile along the shore. At the start point they had a flag on a pole and another buoy out in the water. When she came in line with those two, the boat was supposed to be going at its highest speed. Then when it reached the mile point there was another set of flags. That's how they timed her. The record showed 70.86 m.p.h., but she went faster than that. *We* clocked her at 72.7. For twelve years she was the fastest boat in the world.

"It was quite a thrill for a boy of seventeen. I loved to go out on the flights. Oh, I was paid about fifteen dollars a week. But I would have gone if they'd paid me nothing at all."

Bell himself never rode on the HD-4. "Casey tried to persuade him to take a ride and experience the pleasure," Murdoch Stewart remembers. But although Bell had enjoyed his trip on the Forlanini hydrofoil in Italy, he always declined.

At the opening of a new hydrofoil hall at the Alexander Graham Bell National Historic Park in August 1978, Bell's grandson Melville Grosvenor, who had hitched rides whenever he could, told how he had viewed this hesitation on the part of Grampy with distress. "We thought he was an awful sissy," he recalled. Not so Grammy. "She was always trying to get Casey to take her out and one day Casey did and turned over the controls to her.

There's a photograph taken that day which shows Grampy peering intently out at the HD-4. That was his wife he was watching. When she returned he kissed her and hugged her." Melville added, "Being the same age now as Grampy—more or less—I well understand. I forgive him—now!"

An entry made by Mabel Bell in her husband's notebook for November 11, 1919, describes the experience. "From Spectacle Island I steered the boat almost to the wharf. It was a most wonderful trip, she rose so slowly that I had no sensation of rising, she went just as steadily as a rock. She felt like a rock, so steady, and kept on an even keel. She feels so tight there is no feeling of loose jointedness. She is so stiff and solid. Impossible to feel the least sensation of fear. Occasionally she sort of bubbled as might a smooth going train going over a joint in the rails. I don't call it a bump because a bump means something hard. It seemed to me that it was more on the starboard side than on the other. But it was very slight and rather agreeable to vary the monotony of the perfectly smooth passage over the water. Really the remarkable thing to me was the feeling of perfect confidence she inspired."

By 1920 the Bells were hoping that the HD-4 would also inspire confidence in prospective buyers. Looking for customers, they prepared for visitors from the British Admiralty and the U.S. Department of the Navy.

The famous hydrofoil passing at speed. Two 350-horsepower Liberty airplane motors were used to drive the craft.

Courting the Admiralty

The trials of the HD-4 and the hopes, disappointments, drama, and romance that surrounded the visit of the British Admiralty Commission were made very real for me by the words of Polly MacMechan Dobson. "In the spring of 1920 I decided it was time I left, and I said to Mrs. Bell, 'This year I don't think I'll ... you know ...' and she said, 'Well, if the Admiralty Commission comes out, won't you come back and help entertain?' I said, 'Yes, I will.' I thought it was as remote as Mars because you know what governments are ... they hum and haw. I was actually in Kingston, Ontario, when I got the wire from Mrs. Bell saying the Admiralty Commission was arriving and when could I possibly be at Beinn Bhreagh?

"They were hopeful one of the navies would take the HD-4. Mr. Bell thought as an American he should offer it first to the United States Navy Department, which he did, but the British Admiralty Commission was the first to arrive.

"I got there early to help make arrangements. Mrs. Bell wanted them to have fun besides doing their work. And they did. There were three: G. H. Child, the naval architect and a civilian; Engineer Commander W. S. Mann, who was much older and whom I remembered at once because in the days before we had any Canadian Navy ... perhaps 1906 ... he had been in Halifax with Prince Louis of Battenberg's squadron, which used to spend a good deal of the summers there and had been entertained by my mother. I was a little girl and I suppose a frightful nuisance, always in with the grownups, and he had sent me postcards from China and the different ports he visited; like any child, I was thrilled to get something through the mail. And Tommy ... Commander Claude Congreve Dobson. He was thirty. He got his V.C. [Victoria Cross] in CMBs (coastal motor boats)—small boats that were the forerunners of the motor torpedo boats. They were high-powered motorboats that dashed into harbors. One of the ways the HD-4 was supposed to be useful was as a submarine chaser. With her hydrofoils she could skim over the water.

"Tommy was in command of the attack on Kronstadt in the

169

170

Russian northern waters in 1919. The war with Germany was over, but the war with the Bolsheviks continued. It was a rather romantic sort of thing. Huge Russian warships were in there and it was supposed to be a completely fortified harbor. The admiral in charge of the whole operation said it was so dangerous he wouldn't give a direct order. But they were all young and thrilled with the chance. They went in at night—with the air force bombing and distracting the Russians' attention. They torpedoed three or four of the Russian warships which were a great potential danger to the Allies.

"Every day while the commission was at Beinn Bhreagh they took the HD-4 out for trials . . . probably every day weather permitted. I suppose people were out to watch in Baddeck and everybody who could was out at Beinn Bhreagh. Of course, the HD-4 went at almost unbelievable speed, to us. As she got up speed, she got up on the water and was practically airborne. She had just a little hydrofoil . . . like a ladder with steps of varying width and the last one the smallest . . . skimming along the top of the water. You've seen a dragonfly running across a pond, haven't you? Well, that's exactly what the HD-4 was like. It was very thrilling. Casey always said that the only exciting parts of flying were taking off and landing. So the HD-4 was always exciting because she seemed always just about to take off. Oh, I couldn't believe the speed at which she was going up the bay!

"So that summer they did the trials and it was also the summer that Casey Baldwin and Bill Nutting, an American who was editor of *Motor Boat,* sailed to England in the *Typhoon,* a boat they had built in Mr. Bell's boatyard. They were trying to prove that sailing was not just a rich man's hobby . . . that a well-designed boat could be built on a budget, and they did, in a way, prove their point. They had a following wind and they made England in record time. One of the things Mr. Bell worked on while they were getting the *Typhoon* ready to go over was distilling . . . getting fresh water from salt. It was something he'd thought of and, as he often did, let lie dormant. The fact that Casey and Bill were going on this trip made it a good time to go on with it. I think they did take what he had designed . . . something like a steam kettle with a lot of pipes . . . but I don't think they had to use it.

"The *Typhoon* sailed on July 19, while the Admiralty Commission was still with us. The Admiralty Commission stayed three weeks. Each day after the trial runs, they would go into conference and assess what they had seen. Of course, the members of the Admiralty Commission weren't allowed to show too much how they felt."

Bell was hopeful. On July 10, 1920, he wrote, "The British of-

Opposite page:
Polly MacMechan with her fiancé, Commander C. C. (Tommy) Dobson; V.C., D.S.O.; her parents, Professor and Mrs. Archibald Mac-Mechan; and the Bells at Beinn Bhreagh at the time of her engagement in 1920.

171

At the Dobsons' wedding in Bristol, England, later in 1920, Bell gave the bride away, and his granddaughter Mabel (right of the bride) and secretary Catherine MacKenzie (Bell's right) were bridesmaids.

ficers are observing everything and saying nothing, but I can't help thinking that they must have been impressed with what they saw. . . ." When the officers visited him in his office, there was no doubt about their enthusiasm and interest in his sea-water experiments. "I gave them some distilled water to drink," he noted. And certain other aspects of the Admiralty Commission's visit had clearly been marked with success. "A good deal has happened in the twenty-four days they have been here," Bell wrote on August 2 after the commission's departure. "On Tuesday Commander Dobson paid me a little visit in my study and instead of talking about the trials of the HD-4, he startled me with the announcement of his engagement to Miss MacMechan."

Bell went to England and gave the bride away, but in the end neither the British Admiralty nor the U.S. Department of the Navy took on the HD-4. In due course the U.S. Navy sent a delegation to Beinn Bhreagh and another period of trials interlaced with welcoming entertainment took place. But after the delegation returned to Washington no further word was heard from its members. Only recently, after considerable digging and prodding, was a report unearthed from a dusty dead file in storage. The report was favorable, strongly so, according to Melville Grosvenor, but a top admiral had written across it, "This is an old man's toy: a boat that will not fly."

Today the U.S. Department of the Navy does use hydrofoils. In 1919 the HD-4 was the fastest ship in the world and for many years remained the most advanced craft of its type. Marine engineers benefited greatly from the knowledge acquired by Bell and Baldwin. However, the rough open sea remained a challenge. In 1957 the Canadian Defense Research Board launched a hydrofoil appropriately named the *Bras d'Or*. Sea voyages proved the *Bras d'Or* was not efficient over undulating water; her hydrofoils rapidly succumbed to metal fatigue. Then, in the 1960s, the decade in which the computer came of age, it became possible to change foil positions with great rapidity, and the U.S. Navy is now able to operate the hydrofoil successfully on open seas.

"Yes, Mr. Bell was disappointed they didn't take the HD-4," Polly MacMechan Dobson continued. "Of course, the Canadians eventually built the *Bras d'Or,* the hydrofoil sub-chaser. As they say in Cape Breton—don't be talking! All that that's cost the taxpayers! Of course, it's no more like the HD-4 than I'm like Greta Garbo.

"My husband thought the HD-4 could be successful, and he was very disappointed that the Admiralty didn't take it on. But if you read history, it's always the same. As soon as the war is over, what do they do? They get rid of the armed forces . . . all the weapons they've spent thousands on. No country wants to spend any more money on anything to do with the services. It's swords into plowshares.

"Mr. Bell was indeed surprised by my engagement. The romance proceeded quite quickly . . . the Admiralty Commission was only there three weeks! But I think he was pleased it took place under his roof. I think he was a romantic and in a way a sentimentalist in spite of being such a scientist. That usually doesn't go with sentiment, does it?

"There was one funny thing. When the *Typhoon* arrived in Cowes . . . Casey and Bill had planned to be there for Cowes Week to demonstrate the boat . . . it was early in the morning. They had dropped anchor, and Casey was on deck in a sweater and pyjama trousers and Bill about the same. Facing them was a yacht with two very pretty girls on deck. Casey certainly had an eye and he hailed the yacht and when the girls heard they had just come from Canada, they said, 'Come on over for breakfast.' So they went over and when the girls found out they had come from Baddeck, one said, 'I've just heard from a cousin of mine that he's got engaged to a girl in Baddeck! Can you tell me anything about her?' That was the first Casey and Bill heard of it because of course they had had no communication from the family.

"My mother and I went over to Britain in October, and Tommy and I were married from his mother's house in Bristol. My father couldn't come; he was still professing at the university. Mr. Bell gave me away, and Mabel Grosvenor and Catherine MacKenzie were my bridesmaids.

"One of the things Mr. Bell did while he was in Britain was receive the Freedom of the City of Edinburgh. I really think that honor pleased him more than anything. You know he was a true American. Like any convert, he was more zealous than people born to the faith. He didn't care for the honorary title of 'doctor.' He became more democratic than the most democratic American when he embraced American citizenship, and everybody was more than equal. But receiving the Freedom of the City pleased him terrifically.

"When I was leaving the Point, Mrs. Bell gave a big fancy-dress ball . . . a farewell for me. I remember one thing that I was very proud about: Mrs. Bell's mail was always collected and brought around, and I opened any business things and put the personal things aside for her. There was a letter I could see was business so I opened it, and it was from a girl employed as a secretary in an office in Halifax, saying she had noticed the announcement of my engagement and would like to apply for my place. I took this in to Mrs. Bell, and she read it through and said, 'Polly, write her and say I have no intention of replacing you at the moment. I can think of no one who could take your place.'

"And I don't think she ever did have anyone else, because, you see, Mr. Bell died in 1922. I don't think if you had any medical knowledge you would say his death was sudden because he had anemia and also he was diabetic. His diet had to be watched and he was very naughty about that; he used to like to slip away and eat the things he shouldn't. But his death was so simple and pleasant. He'd had a marvelous life; his family were all there. Mrs. Bell died just five months later. It seems so awful after a death to say, 'Well, it was a blessed release.' But Mrs. Bell was losing her sight; blindness would have cut her off completely. And probably she had no wish to live after he died; it was such a long marriage and time together."

Final Days

The Bells are buried on top of Beinn Bhreagh near where the tower stood. "It breaks my heart to see the tower," Mabel wrote to Casey in July 1922. "Mr. Bell wanted to go there, so we drove there. I won't go again if I can help myself. I can't get it out of my thoughts. I am getting superstitious about it. I feel as if Mr. Bell's life were bound up in it. Can't it be patched somehow?"

But the tower couldn't be patched. Within a month, on August 2, 1922, Alexander Graham Bell died, and two days later was buried in a plain wooden coffin lined with airplane silk. "He had his casket made in his own laboratory and the men who worked there were his pallbearers," Mayme Morrison Brown recalls. "He wanted all that." The women of the Young Ladies' Club met in their homes and made wreaths from the flowers in their gardens. Then a great number from Baddeck walked up the mountain to the funeral. Children like Freddie Pinaud came in their bare feet. The women of the Bell family wore white and Catherine MacDermid, daughter of the captain of the *Blue Hill,* remembers, "Mrs. Bell stood with her hands on the coffin."

Soon after, the tower was taken down.

Daisy was comforted by the fact that her father had had "the most wonderful life anyone could have," as she wrote to her absent sister, Elsie, on the eve of their father's death. Later she felt that her father could have lived longer had he not been so loath to consult physicians, believing in the body's own curative powers. "The anemia, I feel sure, could have been checked and his blood built up. However, then he might have lived longer than Mother—and that would have been far worse."

On the day of her husband's death, in an unfinished letter to Elsie, Mabel wrote, "I am going to carry on the things he was interested in. The HD ranked foremost.... He had a large share in the aeroplane that is successful—he and Casey—but the world does not know it. It must know that he and Casey have built the HD. ..." In the weeks that followed, Mabel found that it was "going to be terrible trying to live without him." But she set affairs in order and wrote an introduction to Bell's last scientific

Opposite page:
Elsie Bell Grosvenor at the grave of her parents. (Gilbert Grosvenor)

paper, "Saving the Six-Nippled Breed," a report on the multi-nippled sheep. And in a black notebook in shaky handwriting she began the story of her life with Alexander Graham Bell, starting with her first meeting with her husband. She wrote only three pages. She lapsed into a coma and died in Washington on January 3, 1923, after having sent to Baddeck for her friend and personal maid, Georgie Haliburton MacLeod, to come to her.

After Mabel's death, Mayme said to Daisy, "It was really a broken heart, wasn't it?" Daisy answered, "Yes, Mayme, it was really a broken heart."

So an era came to an end.

Looking through the pictures of Beinn Bhreagh days, if you're not careful another stereotype rises up in the mind. Beinn Bhreagh becomes the stage set for a big, beautiful, opulent musical (Scottish music!) with the lead roles played by generous, active people—the men all in knickerbockers, the women in big hats and always with kites in hand. But Beinn Bhreagh was better than that. At the turn of the century the Victorians knew a lot and were more secure in their knowledge—Einstein had not yet published *The Meaning of Relativity*—than twentieth-century man would ever be. But none could foretell where their knowledge would lead. Airplanes, space frames, the iron lung, the hydrofoil—all these were in the future, but they could not be predicted. Not all of Bell's ideas panned out; in many cases technology was not ready to absorb them. But at Beinn Bhreagh, Bell sensed the frontiers of knowledge and pushed against them.

For a time the HD-4 lay like salvage on the shore while the kites and artifacts of just under forty years of experiment were stored in the kite house (which the family now dubbed "the museum"). Then Elsie Grosvenor and Daisy Fairchild—Elsie died in 1964 and Daisy in 1962—turned over the hull and most of the museum's contents to the government of Canada. Today the Alexander Graham Bell National Historic Park gives employment to just about the same number that Bell's laboratory did and is another reason why Mabel Bell's expressed opinion still holds true: "Baddeck resembles Washington in one thing: people are always turning up there sooner or later." Alexander Graham Bell still keeps on making things happen.

Old Beinn Bhreagh friends get together with much to talk about. From left to right, Neil MacDermid, Daisy Bell Fairchild, Lexi MacDermid, Effie Stewart, and, on the steps, Helen Stewart, wife of Murdoch Stewart. (About 1950)

Epilogue

You still feel his presence. Baddeck people who loved him speak of him often, giving him life and breath and ready opinion. "I don't know what Dr. Bell would think of trailers," says Mayme Morrison Brown, "but I'll tell you this: he loved any little camping place; he loved anything modern."

I am sitting in the trailer where I have sat during many happy hours. I am checking a few points, asking a few final questions, and Mayme is speaking with the clarity and optimism I admire. "Making the kites was a job I did. I never thought anything of it. Should have, but I didn't.

"It was fun; I enjoyed it."

And watching her fine eyes light up, I have once again a sense of the thrill and the excitement that must have been part of the work at Beinn Bhreagh; that must have been part of the job in the many home workshops where the shattering discoveries of Victorian and Edwardian times took place. Will they ever make movies about inventions devised with the aid of computers in the labs of giant corporations?

"Do you think it's more difficult for the individual to make a contribution today—" I begin.

But Mayme disposes of this dreary question with dispatch. She pulls me up short. As she once told me Alexander Graham Bell could do, she cuts me off at the pockets.

"Oh, there is that," she says, "but he'd try to make the young people be more ambitious. He'd try to get people to follow everything up—the least little thing. You never know where it may lead you."

Can Alexander Graham Bell, as Helen Keller long ago wistfully suggested, show all of us, even in the age of High Tech, how to be inventors?

Perhaps not. But he can show you how to be a generalist.

Opposite page:
Bell watching the HD-4 on a trial run with his wife, Mabel, at the controls. (Gilbert Grosvenor, 1919)

Reference Notes

The photographs in this book are chiefly from the Gilbert H. Grosvenor Collection of Alexander Graham Bell Photographs, presented by the Bell descendants to the Library of Congress as part of the Alexander Graham Bell papers. The collection, assembled by Gilbert H. Grosvenor, Bell's son-in-law, contains early daguerreotypes, portraits by turn-of-the-century professional photographers, and, in family albums and scrapbooks, pictures of Bell and his family in public and private moments. It also contains the remarkable photographic record Bell compiled of the Beinn Bhreagh experiments.

To illustrate specific subject matter, the selection from this rich collection is augmented by a number of photographs from the Notman Photographic Archives, McCord Museum, Montreal, and from the personal collections of those associated with the Bells at Beinn Bhreagh.

The text of the book draws upon two principal sources of material: the author's interviews with various persons associated with Alexander Graham Bell and his family at Beinn Bhreagh and documents in the Alexander Graham Bell papers. Excerpts from the interviews, conducted over a three-year period, are presented here as reportage using the direct quote only. In most cases these conversations were tape-recorded. Naturally, the viewpoints of informants are their own and differing versions of some of the stories related here may exist.

From the Bell papers, extensive use has been made in the text of the reminiscences of Marian (Daisy) Bell Fairchild. The text quotes also from the reminiscences of Elsie May Bell Grosvenor and from those of Charles Thompson.

Quotations from the writings of Alexander Graham Bell and Mabel Hubbard Bell are taken from letters, photograph albums, manuscripts, speeches, and from Bell's journals and notes. Bell wrote daily accounts of his laboratory experiments as well as of his daily activities and thoughts. These appear in the Lab Notes, the Home Notes, Dictated Notes, and the *Beinn Bhreagh Recorder,* a type of in-house newsletter that Bell circulated among friends and associates.

I am grateful to the Canadian Broadcasting Corporation and to The Maritime Telephone and Telegraph Company Limited for permission to publish excerpts from material in their archives.

Sources for direct quotations from the Bell papers, unless supplied in the text, are given below, following the page number and the first words of the paragraph in which they appear. For the sake of brevity, the names of Alexander Graham Bell and Mabel Hubbard Bell have been abbreviated to their initials (A.G.B. and M.H.B.).

Pages

19. (One day in the museum library . . .) A.G.B. to M.H.B., December 12, 1885.

19. ("Oh! Mabel dear . . .") A.G.B. to M.H.B., April 5, 1879.

26. (On a plaque . . .) A.G.B. in a speech before the Patent Congress, April 17, 1891.

31. (Except for . . .) M.H.B. in "The Beinn Bhreagh Estates," notes written for the *Beinn Bhreagh Recorder,* Vol. XV, February 24, 1914.

36. (Daisy was born . . .) A.G.B. to Alexander Melville Bell, February 26, 1880; A.G.B. to Marian (Daisy) Bell Fairchild, February 15, 1901.

38. (Such narrow squeaks . . .) A.G.B. to M.H.B., October 2, 1913; A.G.B. to M.H.B., June 12, 1887; A.G.B. in the *Washington Post,* July 4, 1901.

44. (Mabel had first heard . . .) M.H.B. in unfinished reminiscences.

45. (The Bells had . . .) M.H.B. to Gertrude McCurdy Hubbard, March 6, 1901.

46–48. (During the Bells' . . .) A.G.B. to M.H.B., November 7, 1901.

51–53. (The expenditure . . .) Lilian Grosvenor Jones in "My Grandfather Bell," *The New Yorker,* November 11, 1950.

53. (Mabel Bell handled . . .) M.H.B. to Gilbert Grosvenor, January 29, 1920.

61. (Mabel Bell herself . . .) M.H.B. to Gilbert Grosvenor, May 4, 1922.

64. ("What a prize . . .") A.G.B. in Dictated Notes, October 12, 1901.

67. (His involvement . . .) M.H.B. to A.G.B., December 3, 1889; A.G.B. to M.H.B., May 23, 1887.

72. (Bell's sheep-breeding . . .) M.H.B. in her introduction to "Saving the Six-Nippled Breed" by A.G.B. in the *Journal of Heredity,* 1923.

72–73. (Bell first . . .) A.G.B. to M.H.B., April 19, 1891.

78. (Bell foresaw . . .) A.G.B. in early Home Notes, May 31, 1878.

85. (Bell's interest . . .) A.G.B. in early Home Notes, October 6, 1877.

87. (Bell and Langley . . .) A.G.B. to M.H.B., June 15, 1891; A.G.B. to M.H.B., December 14, 1893.

87. (In 1896 Bell watched . . .) A.G.B. to Samuel Pierpont Langley, May 8, 1896.

87. (But in 1896 . . .) A.G.B. in "Aerial Locomotion," *National Geographic,* January 1907.

89. (Bell picked . . .) A.G.B. to M.H.B., October 25, 1901.

90–91. (In his notes . . .) A.G.B. in Dictated Notes, September 30, 1901.

92. (The construction . . .) M.H.B. to Gertrude McCurdy Hubbard, October 6, 1902.

92. (Each day brought . . .) A.G.B. in Home Notes, November 18, 1902.

92. (Mabel's second . . .) A.G.B. in Home Notes, November 20, 1902.

103. (Bell's conception of . . .) A.G.B. in a speech before the American Philosophical Society, March 7, 1909.

120. (Selfridge had escaped . . .) M.H.B. to Gertrude McCurdy Hubbard, September 22, 1908.

125. (In his notes . . .) A.G.B. in Home Notes, February 23, 1909.

126. (The big kite-plane . . .) M.H.B. to Gertrude McCurdy Hubbard, February 21, 1909.

135. ("Mr. Baldwin is . . .") M.H.B. to Gertrude McCurdy Hubbard, August 16, 1908.

135. (Bell had recorded . . .) A.G.B. in Dictated Notes, September 2, 1901.

138. (Although about to . . .) A.G.B. to M.H.B., June 25, 1911.

138–39. (Domestically . . .) A.G.B. to M.H.B., October 7, 1913; June 15, 1911.

141. (From my house . . .) Barbara Fairchild Muller in a letter and telephone conversation with the author.

146. (On another occasion . . .) Barbara Fairchild Muller in a recorded telephone interview with the author.

150. (The grandchildren . . .) Lilian Grosvenor Jones in a telephone conversation with the author.

150–51. ("I think . . .") Barbara Fairchild Muller in a recorded interview with the author.

166. (An entry made . . .) M.H.B. in Home Notes, November 11, 1919.

171–72. (Bell was . . .) A.G.B. in Home Notes, July 10, 1920; Home Notes, August 2, 1920.

172. (Bell went . . .) Melville Grosvenor in a speech on the occasion of the opening of Hydrofoil Hall at the Alexander Graham Bell National Historic Park, August 1978.

177–79. (On the day . . .) M.H.B. to W. Warren, August 20, 1922.

Bibliography

Blanchard, H. Percy, ed. *The McCurdys of Nova Scotia.* London: The Covenant Publishing Co., 1930.

Brannan, Beverly W., with Thompson, Patricia T. "Alexander Graham Bell: A Photographic Album," *Quarterly Journal of the Library of Congress,* Vol. XXXIV, No. 2, April 1977.

Bruce, Robert V. *Bell: Alexander Graham Bell and the Conquest of Solitude.* Boston: Little, Brown and Co., 1973.

Grosvenor, Lilian. "My Grandfather Bell," *The New Yorker,* November 11, 1950.

Jensen, Oliver, ed. *America's Yesterdays: Images of Our Lost Past Discovered in the Photographic Archives of the Library of Congress.* New York: American Heritage Publishing Co., 1978.

Lash, Joseph P. *Helen and Teacher: The Story of Helen Keller and Anne Sullivan Macy.* New York: Delacorte Press/Seymour Lawrence, 1980.

MacKenzie, Catherine. *Alexander Graham Bell: the Man Who Contracted Space.* Boston, 1928. (New York: Arno Press facsimile reprint of 1928 ed., 1978.)

Parkin, J. H. *Bell and Baldwin.* Toronto: University of Toronto Press, 1964.

Pelham, David. *The Penguin Book of Kites.* New York: Penguin Books, 1976.

Roseberry, C. R. *Glenn Curtiss: Pioneer of Flight.* New York: Doubleday and Co., Inc., 1972.

Waite, Helen E. *Make a Joyful Sound: The Romance of Mabel Hubbard and Alexander Graham Bell.* Philadelphia: Ryerson Press, 1961.

Warner, Charles Dudley. *Baddeck and That Sort of Thing.* Boston: Houghton Mifflin Company, 1874.

Index

Page numbers set in italics refer to captions; however, continuing page references often include captions and photographs within those pages. The relationship of each family member to Alexander Graham Bell is given in parentheses following the name.